#3022

EPILOGUE

Insights into Life
Before and After Death

A CHANNELED BOOK
Jean K. Foster

Distribution by the Talman Company:

The Talman Co., Inc.
150 Fifth Avenue
New York, N.Y. 10011

ISBN # 0-912949-18-X
Library of Congress Catalog Card # 88-051047

A
Uni ★ Sun
BOOK

CONTENTS

Nicole

Tina

Wilma

Orin

Edgar

Etemma

Bob

Peter the Good

Tonya

Edna

Nancy

Bret

Thelma

Ben

Peter, the Entity of Eternal Truth

Thomas

Natural Disasters

Foreword

By Jean K. Foster

"Epilogue" addresses many questions: What happens to our spirit selves when we pass through death? Where do we go? Will we be punished for our wrongdoing? Will we meet God? What will life be like in the next plane?

This book is a compilation of personal stories told by spirit entities who have left the earth plane for the adjoining, interpenetrating plane of life. Each story is an epilogue—a closing comment upon the individual's past lifetime and the adjustment into the next plane of existence.

These stories came as an outgrowth of my search for the truth of God. Advanced spirits called the Brotherhood of God had entered my life at my invitation. They call themselves the counselor, the comforter and the Holy Spirit (communicator), and they help me or anyone to live life successfully. They also help anyone who asks to form a channel to God-mind, that Source of truth open to everyone.*

In my own search for God truth, I asked about the process called death, and I wanted to know about the next plane of life. Therefore, when death came to one I cared about, it seemed most natural to ask about that person's spirit. One day I was told that I could make contact directly. If I needed help or advice in making contact, one of the Brothers named Love promised to come to my assistance.

Each spirit person contacted began with greetings of some kind and a verification of his identity. If the individual had been given to humor in his earth life, his spirit would express humor. Each

*The Trilogy of Truth, by Jean K. Foster: The God-Mind Connection, 1987. The Truth that Goes Unclaimed, 1987. Eternal Gold, 1988. Kansas City, Uni*Sun.

personality I knew on earth presented himself—or herself—as the one I remembered.

I shared some of these epilogues with close friends who found them both interesting and valuable. "Could they be put into a book?" I was asked. Those who have read these stories firmly believe they will be helpful to those who are afraid of death as well as those who grieve over loved ones to the point of despair.

Only a few stories in this book are from people I knew personally in this lifetime. Most came from people I read about in the newspaper. Others were introduced to me by Love, the communication specialist and advanced spirit from the Brotherhood. Everyone told stories that added much information not only about life in the next plane, but life in the here and now of the earth plane.

Some of these spirit entities insisted on knowing why I asked to talk with them. When I explained that the stories were going into a book, each one hoped that his story would help others to live their lives wisely while in the earth plane and to better understand the next plane of life, where all departing spirit entities go after "death."

One epilogue continues through ten installments. I contacted this spirit, along with several others who had committed suicide, and asked him to tell why he had killed himself. As his story unfolded, he asked to stay in contact so that he could explain how his situation developed. More than a little surprised, I agreed. He explains what happened to him after he committed suicide and what he found when he awakened in the next plane of life. He takes the reader through his experiences as he adjusts to his new circumstances, reflects upon his lifetime and finds his way through a maze of erroneous thoughts and heavy emotions to a positive look into his future.

As this series of interviews, called the "Hiram Series," continued, those in the Brotherhood of God became very supportive of this book and especially of the story from this particular spirit who calls himself Hiram. The messenger from the Brotherhood said, "Hiram is our candidate to become the symbol of how those who enter this plane of life can work with advanced spirits to grow and become what all want in truth—to be one with God."

A group of essays are included at the close of the book. These writings cover a number of subjects regarding the next plane of life, and they discuss topics that are relevant to our lives on earth. The material comes from "specialists"—advanced spirits in the next plane.

Introduction

Questions and Answers
About the Next Plane of Life

Other advanced spirits in the next plane of life who call themselves the Brotherhood of God have given answers to questions about what happens after what we call "death."

What is death?

What you name "death" is not the end of you. The reality which is spirit teams up then with what it truly is—the expression of itself as developed in lifetime after lifetime.

What happens when a spirit leaves a body?

Your spirit, which is your reality because it endures, enters the next plane of life where it teams up with a guide who helps you to review your past lifetime. Not everyone wants to team up with a guide at first, but eventually everyone seeks a helper to find better expressions of their spirit selves.

What is our greatest surprise when we leave our bodies?

To enter into this place, so like the earth plane, and openly to produce your thoughts into things.

Do you mean that thought becomes tangible?

Here everyone communicates by thought. They create by thought, and they even get what they need and desire by way of thought. The matter of thought is important if entities want to team up with what is good. Those who enter here in fear, therefore, may reproduce their terrible fears.

EPILOGUE

Will a fear of dying carry over to the next plane?

Only fears of judgment or thoughts of retribution will carry over. Everyone is met by a guide who helps to remove those fearful thoughts of death.

Throughout "Epilogue" there is mention of a guide who meets those who die and enter the next plane. Who is the guide?

One who has advanced in understanding opens himself to help each new tender spirit. This guide or helper comes immediately, comes with greetings, with tenderness, with eternal truth for the newly arrived spirit.

What can we do to be prepared for the second plane of life?

The advanced spirits prefer to prepare each of you individually, but if they cannot do this, then a group method (by way of this book, for example,) may at least help. The best aid is given to each person before he comes here, for in this way the individual will not only be prepared for life here, but he will be able to live a productive lifetime in the earth plane.

Each advanced spirit works with tenderness in the open heart of one newly arrived, but not every spirit has an open heart or an open mind to be able to receive our help.

In what way do the advanced spirits help us?

The only way to explain this is by teaching you how our plane operates. Therefore, team up with us and give your attention to these words.

This plane exists as the one where all spirit entities enter after the earth life is over. It is also the place where spirits gather who prepare to return to earth life one way or another. Therefore, this plane is very busy with the coming and going of spirits. That is why the eternal wisdom of God is needed to get your spirit self into the right eternal truth.

Each spirit comes with some truth within it. That truth may be what is good, or it may be that which is not good. The truth may be that which enters a person from God-mind, or it may be inferior truth from earth-mind. In any case, truth is what a person accepts and believes in.

The guide who greets each spirit wants to help it to acclimate quickly. Many enter here with diverse ideas which need to be sorted out. One of these problem areas is those who enter with preconceived notions.

They say that they know the entire truth of this plane. They give their demands to the guide, but they open their minds to nothing the guide tells them. Their thoughts concern the expectation they bring with them. We can, therefore, do nothing with these spirits until they settle down and admit they actually know nothing at all.

Those who are open to us are ready for learning, and we can team up with them to help them make their own God-mind connection.

Is there any unforgivable sin?

No entering soul will be met with judgment! The erroneous thought that there is a gate of heaven that swings open for only the few is simply not true! The entities who enter here eternalize (project) whatever they expect. That is the first thing that happens. But when they get past this point, they usually let the guides help them go further.

Therefore, entering spirits who have great burdens of what they call "sin" team up with their guides to learn how to reconcile God truth with what they believe. There is no unforgivable sin except on earth. The earth-mind enters many things as unforgivable, but the way of God is not the way of mankind.

In the light of all you have said so far, what advice would you give those in the earth life?

Those who want to live their present lifetimes successfully need the truth that comes only through God-mind to their minds. We can help anyone attain this truth by teaming up with each one who asks us. The way we do this is by helping you to build an open channel straight to God-mind, straight to your perfect truth. When you do this, you will receive not only your perfect truth, but you will also receive the entire message of God. Then you will know how to advance your life into all that you hope for in your heart. Then you will understand the relationship between the earth plane and this plane, between your spirit selves and your body selves. When your time comes to enter this plane in spirit, you will rejoice, for you understand the Pure Truth.

William

1

A man recognized as a successful businessman, a person active in his church and his community, lived over 100 years in the midwest United States. I knew of this man, and a few months after his physical death I asked if I could speak to him. A few seconds elapsed, and then I felt a rush of enthusiastic vibrations as this energetic entity brought me his story.

Team up with William Everett [fictitious name]. The one who entered this plane of life is not dead, and thinking of me as the one who was William Everett is entirely okay. In fact, the name I go by here is William Everett. Since I was on the earth plane for 100 years, I am not ready to abandon that lifetime experience or my name there.

My guide met me and wants me to review the good in my life. Going over all that was good in my life takes awhile, you know. The one who called himself William Everett was pretty good!

Did I detect laughter?

There is much to tell you. This plane of life has no boundaries. By this, I mean that there is no way to know how to stop yourself when you travel. The thought of going somewhere takes me there! Isn't that wonderful?

This new plane is my home for now while I begin to get the truth of my previous life experience. But this will take some time because I lived there a long time, and because, if I do say so myself, I did very well in being the truth in action. There is much to eternalize, and I intend to eternalize every bit of it! [Eternalize as used here means to make permanent and lasting within the individual.]

EPILOGUE

Here William Everett addressed me personally. I have no idea how he knows so much about me, but obviously he knows about The Trilogy of Truth.* At the time I received this communication, I had no publisher.

This truth you write has much to commend it. This truth must get into print, and if I were there with you in earth life, I would get out there and find that publisher for you!

He hesitated a moment or two, and then continued.

The entity who will publish your books will enter the scene soon, I am told. That is good. Meanwhile, I will look around. The truth must flourish.

Get the partnership with these good Brothers every day because they know that what they give to mankind really works. That is the main thing, you know. The truth that really works is worth having. Give it your teamwork each day. Get into the flow of it, and go with it to become the truth that flows into the books and into the bookstores.

This truth enters me, and much of it is new to me. But it is not foreign to me either, in spite of what you might think. The truth is universal, and that means that it appeals to everyone.

Now put yourself to a test! The test is what you understand about this plane of life. The thoughts you send to me seem foggy. That is too bad, but probably it is natural. The truth of the matter is that this plane of life has eternal good everywhere. The earth things, the tender plants, the animals, the people—all those you enjoy, right?

But here, would you believe, they are even better. The place where I am attached, and it does seem to me that I am attached, sort of, has the beauty of environment, of people, of thoughts, of every scene and every good thing.

The one who was my wife on earth, the entity people knew there as my partner, is here too. She gets into the good of this place, grows with the truth of her spirit and grows more beautiful besides.

This one is not my wife here, of course, but this person has the deep feeling that I have, and we stay together here as we did in the earth life. This may not be forever, but it is for as long as we desire this partnership. This plan has the advantage of keeping our lives rather like they were in the earth life, and we therefore make this adjustment better.

The eternalization of what was good in her life is getting well underway now, and she moves with greater speed than

---

**The Trilogy of Truth,* by Jean K. Foster: *The God-Mind Connection,* 1987. *The Truth that Goes Unclaimed,* 1987. *Eternal Gold,* 1988. Kansas City, Uni*Sun.

I do. The thing that I love here is that we have the wonderful love that we had while on earth, but we have none of the problems. Teaming up with good is easy here. That is what I like, teaming up with all the good of the universe.

Tenderness abounds here. While on earth, I tried to express tenderness because I always received so much of it. This understanding eternalizes within me now as the truth that God loved me then and now, has always loved me, probably, and that there is no truth more important than this one. Gentle thoughts waft over me continuously, thoughts that give me new tenderness.

The teaming up you and I do now holds the entity that I was before to help you to hear my message. The person that I was in the earth plane was good, but the person that I AM is the truth within me, and that is what will remain when I have gone over all my lifetime experience. This is my work for now, my entire absorption with what I must do here. The truth of my being is what I must sort out, and 100 years is the time length that I must review.

I asked William if there is anything he might wish to tell those who are still in the earth plane.

No. This plane will open to them as it opened to me. Their lives will unfold, and they will do their best, I assume, to live their lives steadfastly. Therefore, the truth of their beings is what will enter with them to be their permanent greatness. Therefore, what could I say anyway?

"William, have you seen Jesus?"

There have been many great masters who open themselves to us here. These great entities teach us how to open our minds further and how to make use of the truth. They also encourage us to team up with the absolute truth of our souls. Also, they team up with us to enter our space, our tone or vibration to help us advance in knowledge.

This expresses my experience so far, and I enter into it all with great enthusiasm! The experience here is more than I ever hoped for.

I asked, "Do you want someday to return to earth life?"

This has not occurred to me yet. The other lifetime is too much with me. I am the William Everett of Clarkston, Kansas, yet. This is who I am, not the new person, the one who will advance to other planes. There are some who do go on. This is not my time to do such things. I am happy here, happy and working through my lifetime experience.

I thanked him for sharing, and the enthusiastic vibrations slowly withdrew.

3

SPACE SHUTTLE DESTROYED!

2

*On January 28, 1986, I typed these words on my word processor:
"The space shuttle blew up! The ones aboard—how are they?"
The following report came through me from Love, the Brother
who helps me to contact those in the next plane of life.*

New truth enters them now. They who understood the
truth about their space voyage will now get truth about the
spirit.

They were not alone. There were advanced spirits who
were there to guide them when the explosion came. The great
jolt put them into their own individual world of space, and
they received new thoughts when they knew their bodies
were gone.

There they were—teaming up in the sky where they thought
the space craft should be. They were disoriented, but we
helped them to get their thinking straightened out. This sud-
den jolt, when the eternal truth is not in mind, put them
into a temple where they rest and where they get their eternal
truth reinstated.

Give the astronauts time to know what has happened. This
is necessary at first. They will not be left alone, however, nor
without comfort and help.

Those who mourn them have the feeling of oneness with
the body, but the bodies they inhabited are not truly their
realities. That must be understood.

Now the truth will enter them to become the source of
their new energy. The temple that houses them has the best
of truth within it, and the team of astronauts who entered

5

heavenly space together will enter together into new truth together.

Now let them go. That is what we say to those who mourn. They will enter new truth, new dimensions, new lives. The bodies were destroyed because the truth of their machines was not exactly understood. But their new bodies will not destruct.

Those who were astronauts give open minds to their situation as they have been taught to do. They survive and are entering this new life with enthusiasm. They have much to do here. People on earth cannot imagine that this next life is much the preferred one. Therefore, relax and team up with truth, and let those who now enter here go their way.

February 2, five days after the above communication, I was still filled with the emotion of that disaster. Again, I went to the Brother whom I call Love. "I asked you earlier about the seven people in the Challenger space ship. Are they still in the temple where they were receiving help?" There was an immediate reply.

They enter their own places now. They no longer function as a team. The place where we joined them is no more because they put on the truth of their entities.

I struck the question mark several times. What did it mean to "put on the truth of their entities?"

This truth indicates that they no longer have their bodies, the part that was used in their earth lives. The bodies are remembered there on earth, but the astronauts who inhabited them have already let them go. They let go of their earth personalities to become what they really are—their spirit selves. The astronauts have entered into this absorbing new plane of life, although now they remain close to the ones they were with in earth life—friends, family.

This return visit, the mingling of their spirits with those on earth, is usually the first step before they team up with a temple of their own. This temple is where they will concentrate on the business at hand—gaining knowledge of their spirit entities. The temple is where they will work and live, where they will go over their lives there on the earth plane. They will go over the good in their lives, letting it be absorbed by their spirit entities.

Then they will enter into an examination process where they will review those things that did not go right while they were in the earth plane. These will be examined and discussed, if they wish. Then negative memories will be thrown to the wind of the universe to be forgotten, and only the good will be entered into the permanent self. In this way, the spirits of the astronauts will not make the same mistakes in new lives they may live, either here or in another lifetime in the earth plane.

The spirits of the astronauts who are honored on earth take their places here in the tenderness that God has for them and for all spirit entities. Each one will receive the truth of God according to the understanding of each. This way each person unites with that which is needed to team up with the wisdom of the universe.

"Do these spirits attend the memorial services, visit their families and try to comfort them?"

The astronauts who were in the exploding vehicle in space teamed up together for awhile. There they received the ministry of advanced spirits of this plane. After this they had reunions with others here on this plane.

Those on earth were in shock, deep grief, and they would not be open to those spirits who might come to them. Therefore, the good that these spirits might do by going to earth ceremonies is not worth the tremendous energy that it would take away from their present existence.

It wasn't the idea here that they should return for the reasons you mention. The return was to help them to know what had happened, to help them to adjust to the present circumstance, to go on with their living. Those on earth, while templed in great grief, would not be good to be around.

The astronauts who left the earth plane so suddenly will tend to drift back a few times, perhaps, but we hope the transition is to be complete enough that they will now go forward, not backward. Getting the earth plane vibrations will not help the adjustment. But when they get stronger, more acclimated, they will probably return. They will understand then, however, what the lifetime experience was all about. They will also better understand what the other lifetime experiences will be about also.

Our tremendous good truth overwhelms them now, and it pulls them toward our own plane and away from the earth plane. Tenderness surrounds them. The gentle breath of the good teachers touches them to help them become the team who now express individually in the fullness of spirit.

Earnest

3

When someone we care about dies, grief may overwhelm us temporarily. Sometimes it affects us the rest of our lives. I asked Love if some spirit in the next plane would speak of grief and give us some insight into it? There was the slightest of pauses. Then Love answered.

"Grief comes about because those still in the earth plane have no true conception about what death is. They think of death as a 'forever' thing, rather than a temporary transition. The entity who will speak with you now comes to express his own story of how grief hurt him in his earth life."

You may call me Earnest. The one that I am now knows the truth about death and grief, but in my last lifetime I did not find those answers until the explanation came to me when I thought I was dying.

Impressions of a dignified and buoyant personality filled the room.

When I was a child in my last earth life, I entered into grief with the boldness of one deceived. My mother, a good and dear woman who loved me with all her heart, left the earth plane suddenly when the time came for her to leave, but the time did not seem right for me.

I had a fixed idea of the awfulness of God who opened His Door and took my mother. Others fed me this tripe too. They said that God wanted this good woman, and I should be happy. Their words sounded true to me. Therefore, the awfulness of God became cemented in my mind.

The ones who surrounded me were without truth themselves, as was my mother, however dear she was to me. She had not told me of the universal laws, the truth about life never ending, the reality of spirit that spends a short time

9

here in this lifetime, and the great understanding about gentle tenderness that brings everyone together who shares this feeling with one another. The lifetime experience for me, then, was colored not by God's love, but by God's awfulness! *I winced. How many children had shared Earnest's experience?*

My lifetime experience went on, of course, beyond my mother's death, but no one gave me hope for her presence. Then later when I teamed up with a good woman who became my wife in the earth life, I began to receive new truth. "Hey, Earnest," the truth said, "you will never be free to live your life with joy until you understand that you must enter into the truth about yourself."

The truth, of course, is that I was spirit, not flesh only. When this truth began to seep into my being, I began to hope that the one who had been my mother still lived. What I would have given, what I would have paid, to meet this one I loved so fervently!

Then an unexpected thing happened. My lifetime catapulted to a dangerous climax. The plane in which I flew crash landed in trees in a place far from help. The crash killed many, and while we waited, people died all around me. Some died with hope and with resignation. Others died in fear. I watched, unable to help anyone, but I never lost consciousness.

It was then I rose up out of that plane into the sky above the trees into the clouds and above. As I entered into space, I believed my experience to be death, but it was not. My body lived on, transfixed by the scene around me. My spirit, however, soared above the scene. I saw clearly what was happening. Tender helpers gathered about the plane to embrace those spirits who, like myself, soared above the wreck. Those who were unattached (from their bodies) embraced and joined those tender helpers as they left this area. I watched them go.

I waited for my own guide, and finally one of these tender expressions of goodness came to me. "Are you ready, too?" this one asked.

Indecision overcame me, but I said nothing. Yet, the tender helper knew my mind. "It is not finished for you, I think," this one told me. "Help is coming up the mountain now. Go back."

My mind formed questions, but I could not speak. Yet again, the tender helper knew my mind. "No. You have not died. Even when you do, there will be nothing to fear. The

10

one you long for, the one you love, this one will give you her greetings. Ready?"

I nodded dumbly. Thereupon, in the distance, walking toward me was my mother just as I remembered her as a child. Entering into her embrace, however, I knew she was no longer my mother. She was my caring friend, the eager person who wanted me to know her as she really is, not as I remembered her.

"The past is not reality, Earnest. The present is not reality. The only reality is what you are within your being. The spirit, Earnest. That is your reality. Team up with what is of spirit. Hold your mind open. No person in earth knows your truth. Go to the advanced spirits here in this plane who will help you to connect with God who will give you your own truth. Then you will build the greatest reality you can ever imagine."

The lovely spirit kissed me, but not as my mother. I wanted to go away with her, but she shook her head. I remembered another woman, my wife, one whom I loved as much or more than I had ever loved the one who was my mother. She would need me now, for I had much to tell her.

Then I was in my body again, knowing, remembering, not the same as the one who crashed in that plane. The dead bodies no longer horrified me, for I had seen their spirits leaving with gentle guides who came to help. When the men arrived, pain nearly overcame me. But when it seemed too much to bear, I remembered my reality, my spirit self who was obviously much better at life than it had ever been before. Now it had understanding; now it had entering authority about who it was.

When my body healed, I knew no rest until I had gathered my own truth and embarked upon my life in newness of thought. My wife, the one whom I loved beyond all others, honored my explanations and joined me in search of her own truth. When we finally were separated by death—she went first—I waited for her presence, and this one came often to communicate with me and to offer me her guidance and her being which expressed love.

The grief I wasted when my mother died was the optimum expression of ignorance accompanied by other people's optimum expression of ignorance. But when my wife—equally loved—died, the temple of my being shook with joy, for I understood the truth.

This is what I came to tell you that you might enter it into this book—the story of Earnest who learned what eternali-

11

zations to believe in his life. If your readers want to express grief, OK, but eternalize the truth of the situation—that death teams up with what is poor, inferior earth truth. Only the earth passes away. The reality of you enters into its true existence. There is no death, my fellow spirits. There is absolutely no death.

The vibrations had risen as the story progressed until I, too, felt the same thrill of understanding that Earnest had found. When the story ended, the personality withdrew slowly, carefully, as if not to disturb what I was feeling.

Nolan

4

I wanted a spiritual perspective on racial differences, and Love brought Nolan, one who thought one race was superior to another during his last lifetime on earth. Love gave no introduction except to say, "The one you want to speak to is ready to begin."

The entity that I am, the spirit self of one who lived his life believing in racial prejudice, is entering now to speak to you about this matter of race. Enter my name as the one called Nolan.

The I Am of each of us has no eternalization of color. The spirit selves who enter here sure that one race or another is the correct one are disappointed. There is no way to tell which race the spirit self was part of. The truth that enters us, the truth we work with here, is what determines our appearance.

There is no white, no black, no yellow and no brown or red. The entity who relied in earth life on his perceptions of racial color to determine who was of value and who was not is doomed to disappointment in this plane of life.

The teammates I enjoy here are those who have the same perceptions of truth that I have. Whether they were black, brown, red, yellow or white I cannot tell. Therefore, what eternal difference does color make?

The plane that I am in now enjoys much color, but race is nonexistent. What color are we? The prevailing color of one group is determined by their truth which gives all people the same hue—that which is neither one racial color or another.

The so-called skin colors turn to neither a dark nor a pastel, but rather colors flow through the whole spirit self so that each entity is either one hue or another. There is nothing in the earth plane with which to compare our colors. One thing

13

is sure—the growth level is our measure here. We cluster here not according to race, but according to our truth.

We have an opportunity on this plane to review our past lives. When it was my turn, imagine my surprise when I found I had been every color, every nationality! Eternalizing one race, one nationality as superior as I did in the earth plane, was what I had to think about long and hard. What had I learned? Apparently nothing in my last incarnation! But I will try again, and this time I will go back as one of the race I particularly hated. Then I may learn understanding and become one with the truth of the universe that says no entity may think himself better than another because he or she was born into earth life with one skin color or another.

The truth of God enters to be the only truth that may advance your soul. Therefore, to become one with the inferior earth truth only delays the soul's progress. The entity that I was opened to only one point of view—the view of my own race. The teamwork that tried to help me open my mind only resulted in the fear that I might weaken from my position. Therefore, I urged others to take action against the prevailing group who were of the hated color. That way I reinforced what I thought I had to reinforce. But how wrong I was!

The teaming up process here gave me the truth from the perspective of the total lifetime experiences, not just the one experience. What a truth getter I was in my earth life. What I read from selected reading, what I experienced on the level of poor truth constituted my whole truth! How limiting! How entirely false! How foolish!

The thought projection of racial purity entered the idea of pure blood into my earth life. Racial preeminence—this fixed idea brought me the power of negative thought! These ideas held me fast because I would not open my mind to any truth from God-mind. Oh, I heard the inner voices clamoring for my attention!

"Enter into our counsel," they said, "Enter and know the better way!" But I would not heed them. However, they met me on this side without prejudice! Imagine that! They met me with no judgment, no hatred, not even a sigh of disappointment. "Go over your life," they advised me. "Go over your life, and pick out all that was good and worthwhile. You may keep that forever."

There were good things, all right, but they were the result of limited understanding, not what I might have accomplished had I not been so constricted in my thinking. The good took only a short time to go over, for most of it was

14

not true good. It turned sour because the so-called good was often motivated by the hate I held toward another race of people.

The truth enters slowly, I am told here. Though teaming up with those advanced spirits in this plane of life was possible to me while in earth life, I turned instead to the poorest earth truth there is. Now I must learn the lessons of my past lifetime which have delayed my progress in my true life, the one that I live in this and other planes. I must return to earth, I'm told, until I get it right—that race is no teammate to either good or bad, that race is no determination of what is the totality of purity, that race presents nothing except color, that race only confuses the earth existence in order to teach us the greatest lesson of all—that the truth of our beings is what measures growth, not superficial appearances.

This is all that I came to say. There is no more.

Tim

5

Many deaths reported in the media are the result of drug overdoses. I asked to speak to one who died of a drug overdose.
"This entity whom you want is entering the field of the earth plane," Love began. "He is walking toward you with the energy that every spirit has when the completed review of life is accomplished. Here he is now."

This is Tim, the name I had in my last incarnation. In that lifetime I was a part of the drug world. The one that I was then had no understanding of how wasteful it was to become addicted to the drugs that held me in a vise. To tell the truth, I had no free thoughts past the point when I was "hooked." The vast supply of drugs put me into a never-never land of fantasy where I eternalized very little that was positive. The temple of my being was crowded with monsters of my own making, and that is what I lived with.

No amount of love from my parents changed my thoughts into those that might have led me out of that trap. "Trap" is the right name, for I was held there as fast as an animal that enters only to be caught forever. That became my "normal" state while in the earth plane—the trapped psyche that could not evolve into the greatness that God intended me to become.

Life eternalized within me again and again as "hopeless" and as "terrible beyond hope," and therefore, I had not one iota of good expressing within me. Those who reached out for me cried out their love, their concern, their anguish, but my psyche was not able to properly evaluate what they said to me because of "the trap." That is the truth. There was no way they reached me with their words.

17

Never again, I say now! The world of drugs is an idiot's paradise for the physical being who expresses only fears and fantasies and not realities. I entered this plane because I finally shot too much into my veins to withstand the icy feel of death. Actually, I thought I had embarked upon yet another fantasy.

When I first opened my eyes here, I still felt the eternalizations I had felt there—the drugged tremor, the awful thought of impending physical death, the physical energy flowing away, the paralysis, the gaping blackness that I thought was oblivion. These feelings persisted throughout the long period that the gentle guides hovered around me, trying to awaken me to the reality of my being.

When I finally understood that my body was gone, really gone, I mourned because I had nothing to shoot up, nothing to swallow, nothing to put into my physical system to alter my thought process. "You must receive the new truth of your being," someone told me. "This is not earth life. Drugs do not work here. You must face what is with courage."

Never did I think, while in the earth form, that I would ever go beyond the physical, beyond what I could see, touch and so forth. But after my death, I was in what these guides told me was my "reality." What a surprise, and what a disappointment! It meant that I had just wasted a lifetime. The truth swept over me in waves. Shock waves. This was "home." Earth life was my "opportunity to learn."

Then I went into deep remorse and wept endlessly. Those who helped me entered the temple they built so they could watch over me, but they let me weep until I stopped. "No hurry, little tender spirit," they said. "We watch over you and keep you." These spirit entities came and went, while I, almost in a drug stupor, waited and wept while awareness grew within me.

Time means nothing here, so I cannot tell you how long I stayed in this condition. The point is not that of time, but that of the process by which I re-entered this truth that helps me to sort out my lifetime experience. I have now gone over my life, all eighteen years of it. The good did not take long to review, unfortunately. Those years were spent mostly in receiving from others and in taking from others and finally in punishing myself with drugs to become what some said was "like God."

Teaming up with drugs is not entering into the presence of God! That idea was a great lie given to offer hope for a better life. But no one knows better than I what awful con-

18

sequences occur when the "trap" is finally entered. The awful "trap!" It was here that I ended my consciousness. I entered the "trap" and stayed there. Then I died. That was probably good under the circumstances, for I was on the path to ruining my body anyway. And I might, had I gone on, hurt another physical being in satisfying my own needs for drugs.

Now I study truth. Those who teach me take me from where I am. The death I had in the earth life will be hard to erase, for I must in some way pay my debt to the truth.

I stopped the reception to ask what "paying my debt to the truth" meant. Tim answered.

There are laws, you know. The divine and absolute and universal laws which no one may break without paying the debt. The law that I broke was that I wasted my lifetime experience. The law insists that every spirit who takes a body must enter it and care for it with absolute tender expression. God gives us the body to use, to enter into to express the truth of the Universe. But if we waste the opportunity or refuse to care for the body, we must pay back what we have stolen.

"How can anyone pay back a body?"

Paying back is not the expression, perhaps. The expression might better be "put back into order." Therefore, I owe a lifetime of full service not only to the law I broke, but to my fellow travelers, those I hurt along the way.

"In another lifetime must you live out the truth of your being and also make it up to those who were your parents?"

That is partly it. Just one lifetime is pretty optimistic. Perhaps it will take me many lifetimes to pay it back. But since I stole the opportunity from those who were my parents to give and receive love from their son, I must pay them back in kind.

This is the entire picture of where I am and what I am doing. I hope that others may read this and know there is truth for each individual, if one will go after it. These advanced spirits on this plane stay near the earth plane to help those who want to know their truth and who want help in living it. I send that thought to you who read this that you will not do what I did in my last lifetime and waste your opportunity there.

Jordan

6

When a baby dies, parents, family and friends try to reconcile this event with the truth they believe and understand. It is never easy to accept such a death, and therefore, I asked Love to tell of a baby who died.

To my surprise, Love introduced me to Jordan who died soon after birth. "The entity whom you want to speak to is now entering. He was only briefly into the earth plane when his body teamed up with negative thought projections and gave up on life."

I am the one you call Jordan Cirano (fictitious name). I entered my new body (in the earth plane), but I never got into that lifetime, and that is why I have no thoughts on that subject.

Those who enter earth life but then return quickly to this plane have no experience worth mentioning. This is my case. I remember my birth, happiness over the boy being born, those who were my parents resolutely claiming me for their own. That I remember. The trip there had gone well for me, I thought. The open truth was ready to express, but the opportunity disappeared into nothingness.

My parents never knew me. They grieved because they thought of the son they wanted, the son they would never know. But they grieve amiss. Their grief is not for me, for they do not know me. Their grief is for their own hopes and for themselves. Better that they use their time in planning the future together rather than living in the fantasies they create around me.

No one opens to truth of God-mind without getting understanding. And that is what they need to do now. They, however, listen to earth-mind talk, even though they realize

21

there is no happiness, no forward thrust in that kind of truth. They give their attention to that inferior truth instead of going to the truth of God, the truth that is their own.

They keep thinking of their need to express a son. But they need not worry over such things. I am already teaming up with new plans to re-enter life again, but if they persist with these earth-mind thoughts, I will not go to them next time. I want wholesome thoughts from those who turn themselves to the Light -- to God-mind.

The entities in earth life make much over little, I see. The truth of God would tell them quickly that I fare well. Therefore, quit grieving. The infant that I became briefly has nothing to do with my spirit. The spirit is not a baby, too young to care for itself. The baby part is nonexistent. The only baby thought belongs to those who hate to give up what is no longer theirs to have.

This spirit that I am, the one with the permanent truth within me, is ready to return to earth life where I hope to express the truth of my being. There I will claim what is mine to claim, the wonderful evidence of truth in expression. That is my plan. That is my excellently thought-out plan that was developed by me with the help of God-mind.

I stopped the outpouring to ask, "Why do you want to return to earth life when life where you are now is obviously so good?"

Life here is teamed up with all that is good, yes. But I have not earned the right to go forward from this place to advanced planes. I must return to earth life to enter into partnership with a body and work with truth in the outer expression of my life. When I enter with truth, live out my truth, express my truth in every way, I will team up with what is right and good. Then I will return here and be among those who will advance.

"How do you go about choosing your parents?" I asked.

The parents I want are those who will team up with God-mind, but not necessarily those who team up with the church. The parents I want will give tender expressions, good feelings, happiness, and they will express what is important in life, not what is unimportant. This teaming up with parents is most important.

The parents hold the first key. They bring the baby self into being, and they raise it to manage on his or her own. For my next lifetime I will choose parents with more concern than I have ever chosen before. Other lifetimes I merely hurried to get a body, but then I made the mistake of choosing parents who were teamed up with too much negativity.

What a lifetime of problems! They brought problems into their lives because they thought that was what life was all about. They brought grief into their lives because they presented those thoughts into their minds and manifested them in their daily living. It was hard for me to advance beyond their conceptions. This time, however, I will choose more carefully!

I asked if there was any lesson to be learned from this recent birth and subsequent death.

The entities who were my parents undoubtedly had much to learn here. That is why they work through all this hullabaloo with pain. They must learn that those who were born to them have no eternalization of being theirs in the sense of holding property. We who pass on while in baby form take this as a disappointment, but we have no attachment yet.

However, those who were parents hold these impossible pictures in mind—the baby floating in the ether of the next world without anyone to care for it! How ridiculous! We always enter here with a helping guide to open our minds to the state of our beings. Too bad there is not the same awareness in the earth plane where parents who lose their baby entities can see with the clarity of this plane the life where I am now.

I have heard of spirit families who reenter life together. I asked this spirit entity if it had that experience at any time.

"I have not, but I know of others who have entered in the clustering effect. I have no one in particular that I wish to be with, for my intent is to be free to enter into truth in the next lifetime without powerful attachments.

"Have you anything to say to those who want to be parents of babies as yet unborn?"

"Teaming up with a new body is expressed here as the process which opens itself to new truth, not just for the one entering, but for those of you who bring these babies into being," he replied. Those of you who bring babies into expression need the open channel that will open you to God-mind. The truth that will enter you from the great God will team up with your individual spirits. But so many heed no thought of this possibility. Team up with those in this plane who work as advanced spirits. They hover here just to help those in the earth plane to understand truth and to make truth express in their lives.

EPILOGUE

By entering into this divine arrangement, you will express truth wholeheartedly in your life. The babies will enter with health, with great energy, with all that is needed to open them to life in the earth plane. The truth will also eternalize within each of you to bring you into perfect happiness that only the truth of God can bring. That is why I urge you to turn to the open channel and enter into God-mind truth. Turn to the temple within to receive, work with and express truth.

The editor of this book wondered just when it is that the spirit enters the body of an unborn baby. I asked Love about this matter.

"The teaming up of every spirit with the baby body takes place when the baby is entering into the earth life. The one who enters is thrust into that body and journeys into the new world of its materiality."

I mentioned that regressions by way of hypnosis often bring memories of life in the womb.

"Many experiences in the womb must be recorded in the brain which is a physical eternalization of the thinking part of mankind. The baby within the womb needs to record the experiences, perhaps, but the spirit/mind that enters comes with God truth only, not memories of the mother who bore it into the world."

Nicole

7

After hearing from a spirit entity who left the earth plane right after birth, I asked to speak to Nicole, one who died at three months of age.
"The one you named above," Love said, "is the one we have here at hand, one who recently left the earth plane. She will give her observations to you."

I am that one you call Nicole. The baby self of me entered into much trouble and finally gave up. But I never gave up on those I came to be with. Those who were my parents gave me their love, their caring, but eternal good would not focus on my body self.

Now I am in my present spirit life with full understanding of where I am and why I am here. The baby part was physical. The spirit self is no longer a baby, no longer the helpless one. That physical self teamed up with eternalizations that brought trouble to it, and I became very despondent, I'm afraid. The guide tells me that I forgot that my spirit rules the body, and I just lay there and let the physical self get worse without helping it to get well.

Putting aside my body which is no longer with me, I team up now with my guide who is helping me. Even though I had such a short earth life, my plan is to conquer the mistake I made. The body can be made whole if the spirit self takes hold of the matter with authority. This was known to me before birth, but the fact is, I got so involved in taking my thought focus from those around me that I gave no new energy to the body.

Now I give myself a little rest and enter into reflection. The truth that I took with me was not used, and I need to review it all before I return to earth again. The guide met me, helped me to adjust and then brought me here for my reunion with those who are my teammates in this plane of life.

There is no worry here, no tenderness omitted, no truth that is not sufficient, no teeming problems. Those who were my parents grieve, naturally. They did not want me to go out of their sight, but they need not worry over me, the spirit me. This is the part that lives on, of course. That body, though very pretty actually, was not teaming up with the forces of health. Therefore, it had to let me go.

The entity who was my mother opens her mind to the thought of the eternal ether where I might be, but weighing her down is the thought of the body which would not work properly. That thought must be wrested from her mind if she is to find her own proper understanding of my passing.

The one who was my father opens his eyes, too, to the eternal soul that lives on, but he visualizes me as his baby spirit in this new place without those who love me. If only he could see the tenderness with which I am greeted, and if he knew the great truth involved here!

There is no death in reality, only in that which is material. Reality is perfect, and the material tends to enter into disrepair.

If he would be comforted to know that I live and speak and would help him if I could, I'd tell you to go to my earth father posthaste. But there would be no use. He thinks I cannot express thoughts like these, that I am a baby spirit, a cherub floating in the heavenly forces without any parents to love me. Such a fantasy is hard to bear, for it comes from what is earth, not from that which is of God.

Now I go eternally to the Source of all good, the Source of what is utmost in the universe, the Source of what matters most in every plane of life. This is where they will find me, with the Source.

Tina

8

A friend asked that I include a conversation with a spirit entity who, in his or her last incarnation, died of a long and painful illness. Before I asked for such a spirit, I considered what sort of questions I might ask, and I wondered what enlightenment such an epilogue could bring to this book. Since my thoughts are easily read by Love, it was no surprise that this capable spirit had just the right one ready to talk to me.

"The entity that you want is here now," Love began. "This entity entered this plane of life after suffering great pain for many of the earth's months. The spirit self had to rest a long, long time before it could even face the reality of this present place."

My name is Tina. The experience that I had in my last incarnation was only a thought projection of illness, for now I understand that illness would not have been possible had I understood the truth of my being.

The disease entered my body with a virulent childhood illness. After this first sickness left, the new thing persisted within my body. My parents despaired at the beginning. They gave me no hope for good entering my life. They hated the disease; they hated the God who sent it. Therefore, I, too, hated the disease and the God who sent it.

Nothing in my life gave me hope for being cured. Nothing in my life brought me real joy. I suffered because I was expected to suffer. The family and others who surrounded me gave me tenderness. They pitied me; they hoped I'd have a painless death. But none of their thoughts or their words helped me to have any hope on that plane of life.

Those who turned to God for cures thought a miracle might occur. But they truly did not believe in miracles. Neither did

27

EPILOGUE

I. The God who sent the disease prevailed in mind and in thought, of course, until there could be no other concept of God.

I went on for years in that awful state of affairs before I mercifully died. No one regretted my death. They were relieved to have me out of my pain. They were relieved to see me no more, for who can withstand such a piteous appearance? That was what I entered this plane with—relief and a big question of why God had given me the disease.

No one in earth life believed that God did not send the disease. If anyone believed differently, I never heard from that one. The God they all seemed to believe in liked to send suffering to children, I guess. That is what they enacted daily before my eyes. The spirit self within me tried to clear the fog of erroneous earth-mind ideas, but it could not, or did not.

When I graduated to this new plane without the disease, I had the big question of "Why?" Entering with this question brought me face to face with the problem of opening myself to the appearance of evil, which is what I did in the last incarnation. The appearance was our focus, not the reality. The focus extended to the poor truth taught by earth-mind that God is a vindictive person who enters earth to bring certain people great problems.

There were ministers who called my disease a "blessing." They even told my parents that "God must love us very much to give us this great challenge."

What no one said was, "Take up your bed and walk, little girl. Parents, take the tenderness you feel for your child and give it to her truth center—her spirit which has the great energy of the universe which can heal this body."

Had these thoughts been expressed and responded to, I would have begun to act on my own behalf instead of accepting what appearances led us all to believe, that there was no way to be healed.

This story I tell is my own story, of course. I tell it to explain why I entered into this long and terrible illness which led many to the conclusion that God must be either deaf or blind—or uncaring, at the least. The reputation that God got during my experience was entirely what eternalized because of the misunderstanding of what God is.

My job now is to enter into my being the open and remarkable truth of the very great and very broad concept which makes it impossible to limit God as I did before. Then,

28

when I am ready, I will return to life again to use this new concept of God.

One thing I do know about God now that apparently I did not even suspect in earth life is that God is not the entity Who enters one's life to give and then leaves to go about His business. God is not an entity at all in the sense that I am an entity. God is that broad and vast Goodness, that great and pure Tenderness, that true Purity that I never even suspected. God is Principle; God is Wholeness; God IS.

This concept grows within me to become more and more vast. This is the lesson of my last lifetime, and the lesson I never want to have to learn again.

This is what I came to tell you.

Wilma

9

Wilma (fictitious name, as are all names in this book) was brutally murdered. I read about her death in the newspaper, and I wondered how she had come through such a traumatic experience and what effect her murder had upon her spirit in the next plane of life.

Love gave me a brief report.

"The spirit you ask about has not yet opened her eyes here. Teaming up with this one will take more time, I think. Give her the time she needs to rest, to ponder her situation, to become eternalized within our teamwork. Projecting her open thoughts is what we do here to help her.

"This one who rests entered with such vehemence, such teeming anguish that the Brothers here rushed to be with her. She entered with wild eternalizations of fear, and therefore, as she entered, she produced those fearful thoughts. We intervened to help her become entirely peaceful. The wresting of her fears helped her to let the concepts of the murder go. Then she simply dropped off to sleep.

"We teamed up with her to build her a safe place here, a place where we can watch over her and keep her tenderly in our care. Our expressions of loving care enter her slowly, but she is aware of the tenderness that surrounds her. We let her absorb all this without comment for now. We wait for her to rouse and to seek help. Then we will go to her with suggestions."

A few weeks later I asked if I could speak to Wilma. "If she is now awake, would she like to comment upon her life on earth and her present life for this book?"

"The one you want," my communicator began, "is teamed up now with her guide to bring understanding into her entity. Her own being is continually querying to learn what has happened to her, and what will happen next. Wilma wants to enter now and bring her own thoughts to you. Gentleness pervades her being now, gentleness that is part of her spirit."

After a short pause, Wilma began.

EPILOGUE

The thoughts I have now, after teaming up here with my guide, have helped me to work through my truth which I want to demonstrate now. The truth is working within me, but it cannot manifest until I understand how it works.

No one I knew in the past lifetime has come to meet me yet, but that is because I have been working closely with my guide. The spirit who met me and who works with me now eternalizes (projects) for me what I need in this plane of life. But now I must learn how to do this myself. When this happens, I will be able to meet with those who want to be with me once again. But only the spirit who is my guide is here now.

"Do you know why you are in that plane instead of earth plane?"

Oh yes. My guide showed me the truth when I was able to understand. My attacker who wanted money projected his wrath upon those who accepted it. Those who resisted his wrath entered into his plan. Had I turned myself toward him as a God self with power, he would have fled. That method is as yet unknown to me, but they tell me here that it is possible to protect oneself in earth life if one knows the way to use thought.

The one who sent me here by his way of violence wanted me to suffer, but if I had understood the power of thought, I might have forestalled his plan. But that horror is not my fault, of course. It's just that if I had learned my truth better, I could have protected myself.

Now I take for my own the good of my past lifetime. This part is interesting to me, for that which was good often surprises me. Why didn't I see then that the good is not that which I did in the way of helpfulness? Rather, the good is the truth of God that I put into practice.

No, Wilma insisted when my own thought reminded her that she had given much to others.

The good I did I performed out of the bounty that I had— no great thing. But when the truth within me went into the world to perform, I added much of value to the entire earth plane. That is what I have learned here."

"Could you give me some example of what it means to put your truth into the world?"

The energy I collected from God-mind truth was the same energy which I opened to the earth plane. One of these truths concerned gentleness. The person that I was put gentleness into eternal worth by being a good listener, an understanding person.

Also, I have learned that the God of the Universe put me into the world to enact a special plan. While in earth life, I knew I had this plan, knew it was there within me. Therefore, I searched in my spirit for that plan, and then I began to work on it. This plan became clear to me whenever I turned within to find it. That is the way it came about that I chose the husband I did, had the children I did, entered the work that I did. The plan was what I came to earth with, I realize now, but of course I did not know this while I was in the human body. But yet I performed the plan because this thought was teamed up within me.

I asked Wilma if she forgave her murderer.

He will enter here with his own problems to work out, and I need not enact them myself. If his problems take on too great an importance, I am trapped within them myself. That truth has already reached me.

"How do you feel about leaving your lifetime so unexpectedly?"

By teaming up with my guide, I am learning much. The unexpected entry is interesting. No, I did not expect that day to depart on the train that took me here. That train gave me a ride I had not sought. But yet, it is all right now because I understand that my life there was only a short term plan anyway. I actually had no further plan. The tender truth of God-mind would have had to reach me, and I do not know if that would have been possible.

"Murder is a terrible, violent act. Those who loved you in the earth plane must mourn your death with an especially awesome grief. What would you say to them?"

Never think I am without hope here. Those who met me helped me immediately. Those who team up with me here encourage me beyond all the ways those in the earth plane ever encouraged me. This plane is "home." The earth plane is the far place where I went to express more truth than I had ever expressed before in other places, other lifetimes.

Why enter into continued mourning? My death is over now. The entity who hastened it is now paying in earth terms. Those who loved me there love the one they remember, not the real entity whom they do not know.

"Do you still love them?"

Those I love very much enter their truth to me whenever I open myself to them. Their love is mine here as well as there. Nothing changes the reality. They are learning this part. They enter here whenever they meditate or sleep, and then we talk. That way their grief abates and they feel they are getting their messages to me. And they are.

"Is there anything else you want to say here?"

No. The teamwork with those on this plane is my main concern now. I came without enough wisdom in the spirit. But entering by way of violence does not keep me from progressing as I would have even had I died an easy death.

Orin

10

Since I included an epilogue from the spirit of a woman who was murdered, I now include a story from one who, in his past lifetime, killed and robbed. Love brought this spirit and asked him to talk with me.

The Brother named Love began, "The one you want is ready to give you his own message. He wishes to add a postscript to his life."

When I lived in the earth plane, I visualized the world as that which was to give me all that I wanted, and that is the way I lived. I was not conscious of eternal truth within me. Now I know that I went through a life experience on earth for the purpose of learning that God is the source of all. However, I believed that the earth owed me its bounty, not that bounty came through God.

This belief developed within me because I entered my life experience without taking into regard who my parents would be. I chose unwisely. Those who brought me into the world never wanted me, nor did they ever take me to their hearts. The nature of love as expressed in the earth plane was unknown to me when I went through the baby period.

By the time I grew into a boy, I knew what I wanted—revenge upon all those who hurt me and revenge upon all those who would hurt me if they could. That took in the whole world, I guess.

Eternalizing my own wishes was not a positive projection, for I focused only on inferior thought from earth. That, along with my revenge attitude, brought me into criminal activity. I simply enacted what I put into my mind—what I believed life was all about.

35

No one entered my life to give me a new perspective. That might not have been possible, I admit. My lifetime became the obscene thought form of teaming up with what is entirely too gross to give in detail. There was no goodness in my thoughts. The observer in me refused to let the body enact even one kindness because that observer (my spirit entity) had chosen the path of resistance to good (God). Therefore, no amount of debasing of my body or no amount of debasing others ever satisfied me. Those acts only called for more of the same.

Why? Well, I'll tell you why. When a being teams up with what is entirely the opposite of good, he or she opens to the truth of earth that says, "If you try hard enough, you will succeed." I wanted to succeed at becoming the one who held power over others, the one who could have material wealth at command, the one who would find gratification in all that he took and all that he did in the name of self-satisfaction.

But what I did was to team up with what is untrue—error thinking. There was no satisfaction—ever! There was no sense of accomplishment in anything I did—not the murders, not in teaming up with others to rob and to abuse. The energy I spent in those activities gave me no advantage. The truth of my own being that I had created, that I had built brick by brick, was not the stuff of satisfaction or happiness. Quite the opposite.

No one who is consumed by thoughts full of the teachings of earth, the teachings of ego, the teachings of whatever passes by the mind, can know eternal satisfaction or eternal happiness. What a waste I made of my lifetime experience!

And here I am, like all other spirit entities, without the material things I left behind, and here I am unlike many entities, not even able to manifest the things I want here. The truth eludes me here because I have no "ear" for it. I do not mean I am deaf! I just have no ear for the music played in this plane. Understand?

The optimum presence of good is the eternalization that I want to capture. This is what I work with here. But the experience from earth lingers still, and I try to steal from others to no advantage. There is no possibility here of taking things that others have, and do you know why? There is nothing to be had unless you know how to use thought. The only thought that works here is the kind that works in co-operation with the law of the land, and the law says that no one manifests good unless he opens himself to God truth.

Where does that leave me? Nowhere.

How does that put me into the greatness I long to have? It doesn't.

How can I change all this? By teaming up with the forces of universal energy which operate on the principle of great goodness. How ironic! How teamed up with what I always— in earth life—ridiculed!

No, all is not lost yet. Here I am unable to make it up to those I wronged. The only way I can make my wrongs right is to get into the flow of truth. I have helpers, but they have had a hard time with me. For awhile I joined others like me and left my helpers outside. I wanted to work on my own, in my own way. The stubborn and unloving spirit self persisted. But nothing could be worse than to be in with others like myself. How wet was the atmosphere, how stormy were the days. Our thoughts teamed us up with everything that reeked of great, unfulfilled passion!

Now I have left this place, knowing there must be a better way. And here I am waiting with my helper to get my spirit self into positive action. The one who helps me says I have made progress by saying all this, by understanding what my lifetime experience was all about. This guide says that now I am ready to progress! That is good. That is what I want beyond all other wants! This is the super message I have awaited, and you are here to receive it along with me!

The entity which I am is not lost forever. There is redemption after all. There is hope. There is a way by which I may again redeem the good to my spirit. There is hope that I may go forth again into earth life—this time with more insight, more understanding, and much, much more caution! The world empties its truth upon those who live there, and the only way to hold out against it is to make the spirit strong with its own truth. This is my plan.

I did not enter my name because I am ashamed of it. But give my name as Tender Truth Trying to Express. Too long? Then call me Orin, the one who opens to Truth.

Edgar

11

I asked Love if I could speak to one who was a policeman in his recent lifetime, one who could give us an insight into what his work meant to him?

Love replied, "The one you want is here to review his lifetime experience, and he is now ready to speak to you. This one refers to his past lifetime as that which intended good but which brought forth the projection of what was not good. The patrolman who died while on duty had no understanding of who his attacker was or why he shot the gun. He wants your personal teamwork here to help him with the explanation of what he now believes was important about his life."

I assured Love and the one who was a patrolman that I would give my thoughtful attention to what was said.

"Then enter this one as Edgar, the one who intended good."

The one who I was on earth portrayed my death over and over again in my thoughts. I projected this picture energetically. Therefore, I should not have been surprised that I was shot and killed unexpectedly. I teamed up with this projection many years before.

I know now that it would have been possible to thwart the would-be assassin, but the operating philosopy I held within me did not help me to realize there could be a better way. My problem was my projection of just what happened.

Being a patrolman helped me to see life at its worst, unfortunately. I began to think that this poor picture of life and of those I saw represented most of what the earth plane offered. The tenderness that I once held within hardened and teamed up with wrong beliefs.

39

EPILOGUE

To put any truth into the earth plane, one must open himself to the potential of good. But I closed that energy off by firmly turning away from any projection of good. If I had held to the good—that is, my God self expressing—then I could have thwarted the entire episode that resulted in my death. God truth showed me the eternalization that I might have held in the place of the one that projected my fears.

However, the perfect truth I received seemed too ridiculous to pay attention to. Why? Because the truth that teamed up with me was not subject to reason, as earth-mind explains reason. Teaming up with Pure Truth that God gives is not unreasonable, but when I rationalized it the way earth-mind told me to, then the energy ran out.

The way I thought things worked was that in earth there were things that even God knew nothing about. How could God know, I asked myself, about the terrible depravity, for example? The wrong truth poured into me in this fashion until I put God into one compartment and the terrible things I dealt with into the other compartment. That meant that I could not determine any sort of unified picture of life.

To be a policeman, I thought that I must hold earth truth before me like a lamp. To hold up any possibility of truth that enters this plane through God was hardly the kind of idea that we (I and the people with whom I worked) could tolerate.

Why team up with earth-mind energy? This question is what I ponder now. Why did I think that earth-mind entered better truth than God? This question is what I think on night and day!

Work—my particular work—was that which demanded the best truth I knew, but instead I chose the second, the poor truth that has always led people astray.

Now the person that I was recognizes the one that I am—the spirit self. With this recognition comes an understanding of what my life was meant to present. Yes, my life was lived to put the good that I knew within the earth. But that is not what I did. No—I put the evil into the world by giving it power in my life experience and in the books that record my story.

I asked what books he was talking about.

Those that record my experience, my teaming up with one who killed me.

"But you are considered a martyr, not one who is shamed in any way." His tone did not change, however.

40

The one who shot his gun telegraphed his acts. I heard the message even as I stopped the car. The one I eternalized as the one who had my destiny in his hands presented his poor truth, and I, without trying to forstall it, bought the entire package.

Somehow, I felt that this spirit entity had blown his story out of proportion, that he felt guilty when he should not. I sat there filled with the seriousness of his message and my own thoughts of the person who killed the patrolman. Edgar's words came again.

Team up with what I tell you, Truth-Giver. The one in the earth plane must know he or she can indeed hold the body in protection! Why turn away from this truth? Why eternalize me as one who could not help what happened? Especially when it is not true. I could have turned the deed into one of tender mercy, tender expression of understanding, but I did not.

Enter what I have given you, not what you want to give. This epilogue is mine own to give, not yours to restate. The words that tell it will be mine, not yours. Therefore, hold this message as it is, not as you want it.

And that is what I have done here. I have given the message as he told it, though I stand amazed at the difference in his perception of his death and the perception of those in the earth plane who believe he was a martyr for the cause of law and order.

Etemma

12

*Could I speak to one who had a poor marriage relationship in the
last lifetime? Perhaps this individual might help us to understand
why our poor relationships hurt us so much. Also, what is the
spiritual significance of a poor relationship?*

*"The one who can best describe what you seek is now approach-
ing," Love said. "This individual has now returned to earth many
times to get the personal relationships in order. The way appears
easy when this one looks at it here, but whenever this one has gone
to earth to enter into a new life experience, the eternal truth seems
to enter into oblivion.*

"Call this one Etemma, the woman who loves too much."

The entity who I am is named Etemma. The eternal truth
is what I work with in this plane, the truth that will help me
to become the one I wish to be—the truth that expresses
perfectly.

The last lifetime has not yet dissipated from my mind,
however, because I put my truth into hiding somewhere and
took only earth-mind truth as my guide. The truth of that
mind is fallible to the extreme, and yet I held it within me
as the perfect process by which I would be the best that I
could be.

Here is how it worked for me. The woman that I was in
earth life was quite lovely to view. The perfect complexion,
the wonderful body, the ethereal appearance that belied my
earth truth which expressed through me. Those who knew
me said I looked like an angel, but in reality, the angel part
was of the imagination.

The first man I married had no sense at all. He thought
that because I looked like an angel, that I was. Was he in for

a surprise! This man held me tenderly, and he expected nothing from me except love. The truth in me, however, expected much of him—too much, in fact. This man was not able to satisfy my wants, and that which I poured onto his head from earth-mind was insulting and given to hateful remarks.

This man finally left me, unable to stand my diatribe against him. Then came my next husband. This one had money, but he was hard and hurtful. The entering truth told me to get his money and leave him, and that I did. The way he hurt me, however, was to make me his object of hateful acts. He injured me by teaming up with others to bring hurt into my life. He could not think of anything too terrible to do to me. That ended when, in a fit of anger, he died.

But I, who had no wealth of my own, teamed up with miserable entities there on earth and became the onerous projection of truth gone totally wrong. That is when I died—the result of my poor attachments to those who had no sense of the good or the greatness that God IS.

Entering this plane of being, I tendered my attention upon the one who had been my second husband, for he was there when I entered. This one had died in hate, you see, and therefore, he attached himself to me. This attachment is hard to explain, but if you would think of the hate toward me, which I reciprocated, as a blending of spirits, then you may understand that this hate locks us together until it is somehow dissipated.

This hate is still with me; we are interlocked here in this plane in a quest for finding a way to separate and going our own ways. This spirit of my second husband, however, holds onto that part of me that hates him, and we thrash about without giving release.

Of course this is an unhappy picture I present, but since the writer sought a story of marriages that were not happy, I am asked to give my story. The truth that enters me now may help me to release this one who clings to me. The way he tenaciously holds onto me, I know his own hate has not abated.

The writer wonders when, if ever, I'll be able to go to the earth plane again. The way that I will get my release will be to work with truth, and when I am released, I will try again to have an earth experience that will, indeed, hold the relationships between me and others as that which must be teamed up with truth that enters through God-mind. The selfish thoughts held up by earth-mind only bring disappointment.

I asked Etemma why Love called her "the woman who loves too much." She responded this way.

The answer may not be clear to you. I don't know. But I will try to explain. Truth that enters me now through God-mind explains that there is tenderness that is the perfect blend of qualities that God has as a gift for me and others. This gift is mine even now, and I can feel this God tenderness expanding my better truth into the person I want to be. This tenderness is what I want and need, and I long to hold it within me forever. This tenderness thrusts itself at me, and I grab it and hold on until the teachers come to tell me to let go.

They say to me, "Let go, Etemma. Enter into the tenderness with no grasping, no holding on too tightly. This wonderful tenderness is always there for you. This tenderness will not dissipate nor disappear. Enter into it with relaxed thought."

But yet I still cling as if this tenderness is my lifeline to hope for bettering my spirit self. Therefore, they gently tell me that I love too well! But I know they want to help me, these who guide me in this plane, and I am trying to be more relaxed about this perfect tenderness that teams up with me.

Bob

13

Who could speak to us about love—marriage—good relationships? In this earth plane we invest much of ourselves in creating and keeping love relationships. Of what spiritual significance are these relationships?

"A person who wants a partner—male or female—must put on his mantle of Pure Truth," said the advanced spirit who helps me gather these epilogues. "That is, he or she must gain the truth that enlightens his soul concerning the individual growth plan.

"Each person comes to earth with a plan, though many never enact it. The way to bring your plan into enactment is to surround yourself with those who join you in that plan. Then the law of the universe works on your behalf to have a relationship with another that is of the highest destiny.

"The one who now enters to explain all this comes because he had a fine relationship in his last earth life. He will explain how this relationship developed, why it developed and how they proceeded through life together to open the doors to success for one another."

My name is Bob. Love believes that my own story will be helpful to your book. We here in this plane have the opportunity to go back over our lives, and thus it is that I can offer to you the experience that provided me with the greatest comfort in my earth life.

I began early in life to receive truth that told me I had a definite plan for my lifetime experience. I knew that I must put God truth in motion—that is, I must demonstrate God truth in my life. Therefore, I held to that plan as I made decisions concerning my life. The truth I received clearly projected a plan by which I could enjoy the wonders of nature and at the same time enjoy the kind of life I most wanted. I

47

became one who brought eternal truth to people about our earth—its problems, its needs. I studied the earth, its balance, its union with itself.

I broke into the communication to ask what "union with itself" means.

Union with itself refers to the gentle being which is at the heart of earth, its spirit self. This is the teacher I went to, the teacher from whom I learned. The wonder that was revealed to me gave me the courage to try to change the way the forests were handled. The way I did this is unimportant here, but the reason I was able to do what I did is the choice of my perfect mate, the woman I called Penelope.

She came to my attention when we were both quite young. My head was certainly turned by her beauty, but I knew that beauty alone would never take me to my goals. I held off in my decision until my own entering truth gave me the true picture of the one whom I admired. The truth held her up as energy that teamed up well with me, the eternal good that vibrated with my own good. I could feel those vibrations when I pictured her within my spirit. The two pictures—hers and mine—melted into one another and became the tender expression of beauty. I knew then that her physical beauty was not why I wanted her to be my own. It was her great compatibility with my own being that was the source of my attraction.

Wedding her was the best thing that I did toward implanting my truth in the purpose and plan I took to earth. The certainty of our compatibility was the strength and teamwork that two earth plane people need to make two spirits express their truth.

Now I want to explain that Penelope and I had a strong relationship because we were united in our plan and united in our vibrations. We knew that our situation was unusual, for there were many who could not get along with one another. We did not know then the spiritual why's and wherefore's of choosing a mate, but when we came to this plane, we reviewed the situation. Then we understood why we had a great relationship and why others did not.

My plan was to put good into the earth, and I stayed with it my entire life. By my side was Penelope who also wanted the truth instated within the earth and in the hearts of mankind that the earth must be given respect. We both knew its truth -- that the spirit of the God of the Universe dwells within planet earth, and it is that spirit that we can enter into and learn the secrets of earth's survival and its creativity. It is also that spirit with whom we can communicate to learn how to wrest what we need from the earth without hurting it.

Now you have our story concerning love and the operation of the truth principle of bringing the one you admire within your being to learn the growth plan that is either compatible or not compatible with your own.

Peter the Good

14

Is there anyone else who might speak to us about the love relationship between men and women—someone who might teach us the significance of such a relationship?

Love, the spirit who works with me in contacting those who tell their stories for this book, answered. "The one who enters now comes to tell you his own story, his own personal tale concerning the partnership between his wife and him, a partnership of much tenderness. Their relationship is the perfect example of the eternal truth that those who want a perfect alliance together must concentrate on compatibility in the spirit, not compatibility in the flesh. The flesh, unfortunately, is not stable. The flesh is temporary. But the spirit is the reality of each of us and remains that certain gauge by which we can judge the proper selection of our mate. Here is the one we call Peter the Good."

I asked Peter why he was called "the Good."

The entering truth that God gave me in my last lifetime was put into the earth to help others and to enter into the perfection that God has planned. Therefore, "the Good" means simply that I gained my goals—those which were set before I entered my lifetime experience.

The story I tell you now is a true account, and you must know it as such. The truth that applies to my story is the same truth that can apply to anyone because it is eternal.

The way I became the truth in motion in my last lifetime was by applying eternal truth to finding a wife. The one I wanted was in my mind, but I could not see her anywhere on earth. The one I wanted was energetic with the energy that brings goodness into being, the energy that opens to

51

others to help the truth become matter. Though she was clearly in my mind, I was not sure she existed.

But the thought waves I sent out were not to be denied. These vibrations sent out their signals, their tender messages of desire and God truth that wanted manifestation.

The way it works is that any of us may go into our inner selves to team up with the God truth that is there for the taking. Eternal truth is just that—truth that is there to take, to use and put into the earth. This truth says that if I eternalize (hold a picture in my mind) of what I want or need, then I may produce this truth in the earth plane.

Therefore, I held the woman of my dreams in my eternalization. This kind of picturing may team up with the vibrations that will bring anyone whatever it is he or she holds in mind. That was the way it worked for me. The woman I had pictured entered into my own temple and introduced herself. Then I knew she existed, but where to find her?

My own personal truth from God told me the one I sought could be found in the building where I worked. I didn't know her face, but I began to search. The way I recognized her was by her voice and what she said to me.

"I wondered when you would come," she said. "I knew that there was one man in this company who wanted to contact me, but I didn't know what he looked like."

We understood what had happened, and we began to get acquainted. Our wonderful relationship led us both into the truth that could be demonstrated because we each had the means, the understanding, the entering truth that could lead us to express what we eternalized into the earth plane. That we loved one another was certain before we met on earth. We had worked together before as a team—in another lifetime. This time we knew whom we sought, and there we were, in tandem again.

The significance of the relationship is that when two people who team up to produce their growth plans get the operating truth instated within them, they can then translate their truth into matter, into the earth plane where it will help others. We worked together to help others learn about and enter into God truth, and we worked in cooperation and in tender acclaim for one another.

To become your potential takes every bit of encouragement you can find in the earth plane. To put your growth plan into operation and to reach its perfection takes the friends and the mate who stand by your side. That is why the perfect union between men and women is necessary if they are to arrive at their desired success.

To enter into relationships that earth truth promotes is to arrive at the heavenly kingdom with your team ready to go to work and then buying a ticket for another place because the kingdom is not attainable by those who work with you. Go to the heavenly kingdom—the earth plane where you enter into God truth—with those who know how to attain the kingdom, not with those who will not or cannot enter.

This is my story, and it is my own validated evidence of what perfect teamwork can do to put you into the role of one who attains truth and puts it into the earth plane.

Tonya

15

A person who read some of the epilogues wants to know the spiritual significance of violent jealousy, infidelity, depraved sexual appetites like incest or rape or child molestation. Is there one who could speak of such things?

"The one who is open to your question," Love said, "was herself one of those who entered into most of what you mention. This one, you must understand, has only found answers that apply to her own being, and that is the way it is here in this plane. When entities seek answers, they review their own lives and then seek answers for their behavior. This answer, however, will show insight into the reasons why people team up with what we call here the worst of earth truth, and why they enact it in their precious lifetime experience."

The one that I AM, the entity who is now eternalizing her last lifetime experience, is no longer teamed up with what happened then. The one that I AM is now into greater truth, greater understanding, greater teamwork. You may enter my name as Tonya, the entity who now teaches others. I AM the one who enters into open truth.

The question you focus me on is hard to bear, for now I hate what I teamed up with in the last earth life. But that you might enter the truth into your book, I will comment on the terrible earth truth that took me into eternal blasphemy.

This blasphemy took the form of pure hate on my part of whatever was good in others. The good that I saw teamed up in my mind as falseness that paraded before my eyes, tenderness that was pretense, not real. Therefore, I set out to prove my point. When you decide in earth life to prove your point, the entire practice of your life is affected.

This writer fears I will take her emotionally into my being as it was then. She knows that to descend with me into the pits of my earth despair is to team up with what I then felt and then believed. However, she must "let go" of her offending opinions if I am to release what I have to give.

My life took this form: My husband, who appeared good and brave, was called to be a man of God. That entering truth took his heart and took his time. The way I saw it, he was being not only neglectful, but he was being untrue to our marriage vows. Therefore, I decided to find out just how strong this so-called wonderful man was.

The one I cooperated with was the pastor of another church who thought my husband's decision was good, but he also thought my husband was not thinking of me as he should. I went to this pastor, with my husband's good opinion, and there I teamed up with this pastor to have an affair. It was fun, I thought, really great! And the funny thing was that I got pregnant. The baby had to be my lover's baby because my husband was unable to give himself sexually while he was in the throes of his "wonderful religious experience."

My husband was stunned. Sometimes he wanted to know answers, and sometimes he wanted me to say nothing. He went to a friend for advice—the pastor who had counseled me. Then he realized that the pastor and I had been lovers. He went into shock. He cried aloud and blamed his impotence. Then he blamed the pastor who "counseled" me. The result was a baby boy that I brought into the world as my husband's.

My husband took the baby as his own and demanded that I never see the pastor again. This was my decision, too, my great relief, in fact. But as the boy grew, I entered into another affair, this time with one who teamed up with my husband to bring a revival to our church. This man projected his own personality to me, saw my enchantment, saw my willingness, and I then secretly met him for a wonderful affair. The result was another baby. The husband that I had knew no tenderness for me then. He ranted and raved; he wanted to know who the father was. This time he could only guess, for he could not figure it out.

The two children were thought to be my husband's children, and he tried to pretend they were. But then his truth cracked, and he became full of hate and violence. I enjoyed these emotions, for I wanted him to express himself in this manner. Then I taunted him about all the sermons he had given, the great messages of love, hope, of great concern for humanity.

He became violent toward the children, demanded their obedience on all points, their teamwork with the church, their tenderness for God but their hate for me. He told them they had not been fathered by him, that they each had a different father. The boys, teenagers, turned hate toward me, too. Then I saw that what I had thought they were—simple and sweet—was a facade, and I determined to show those boys that their mother was what people are in reality.

The next part is not easy to give to the writer who recoils in her dislike. I even tempted and had sexual intercourse with both sons. They resisted at first, but I told them they must know about such things, for the one whom they looked to as father would never tell them. He had not had sex for many years. My sons changed toward me soon afterwards. They slapped me, kicked me, teamed up to humiliate me. But yet they crept to my bed to again have sex. They went into great eternal hate of me, and together they conspired to kill me. That is how I died.

The way I see all that I did is that I could not enter into the truth that God-mind brings. The worst earth-mind truth crowded my mind. As I grew up, I learned that I could get whatever I wanted through gratifying men with sex. The first one was my father. He opened his heart to me and loved me, and I urged him to enter me physically. The man tried to refuse me, but he gave in. The sexual relationship went on through many, many years, even into my marriage until my father one day killed himself.

The truth here is that I never did get God-mind truth instilled within me. I saw life as gratification—get my own way, enjoy whatever I wished, team up with whatever gave me pleasure. Those who appeared to have thoughts that I then interpreted as "goody-goody" or "too good to be true" had to be wrong, had to be unmasked.

If there were a "hell," I would have gone there. There was, instead, a teeming life here that I plunged into without any understanding. Tenderness overwhelmed me, for I had never accepted tenderness as real. There I basked until one day my guide asked me to embark upon a learning expedition. I refused, at first, to go. The old earth-mind thinking still entered my thinking. But when I moved about on my own, I saw that life here is not what it was on earth—yet, it is exactly what it was on earth.

This apparent contradiction is explained as whatever I found here, I had brought along with me. The first thing I noticed was that a mass of some substance clung to me without hope of letting go. I picked at it; I asked others to help me, but no one could pull it away.

"You are heavy with your earth life," one told me. "You must get help. That which holds onto you is the stuff you made before you came." I turned to find help, but my guide was no longer nearby. Where had this one gone? Then another entity, one who also had a heavy substance upon his being, came to me with smiles all round.

"Come with me, my tender piece of awfulness, come with me to the place where you will enjoy life."

I quickly went along, and there I entered into a world of people like myself. They all had the heavy substance, and they took turns picking the stuff away from one another. I shivered! The place resembled a monkey pen I had seen once at a poorly kept zoo. The place seemed full of unkempt people, and it was then I knew I looked that way, too. Where had my good looks gone? Where were my satisfactions?

This group encouraged me to tell about my lifetime experience, and they applauded as I told them what happened. Their faces held no tenderness or caring. Instead, they held expressions of lust, of greed, of desire, of hunger, of wanting more and more but never being satisfied. I stayed there for a long time, going over and over my lifetime experience, and I listened to the lifetime experiences of others. Then I began to wail in great unhappiness, and someone threw me out a door into a turbulence of vibrations that tumbled me about so I had no rest or quietness.

In the distance I saw the one who had tried to help me much earlier, and I called out. This one came and the turbulence quieted, and he took me into his arms to wipe my tears and to give me hope that I could gently work to give myself new enlightenment.

That is where I am now. Better stories than this one are, no doubt, yours to present. There is no happy dream fulfilled, no goodness instated anywhere, but the meaning is apparent that those who give themselves over to earth-mind truth build around themselves a ball of hard and unyielding substance that they will bring with them into this plane.

The wonderful truth that I am now learning will be mine when I again return to earth life and when I enact God truth in my lifetime experience. There is nothing I can do about the ones I dealt with so badly in my last earth experience.

That I may meet them again is possible, for I have left so much undone. But if and when we meet is not certain.

The writer asks me about karma, but I have not yet heard anything about this. That I may have to repay in kind in some way is possible, but I am working now to release the emotions that held me bound to those I hurt. The karma eternalizes as that which is possible, but which need not be.

The writer wonders if there is anything else I have to say, but there is not. The one who wanted to unfold this kind of story asked the writer to do this. She entered the request, and now here it is. There is no more.

Edna
16

Mental illness—a catch-all term for many mental problems—is addressed in this epilogue by one who tried to live in the earth plane with her mind full of contradictions and misunderstandings. A postscript to this story is given by an advanced spirit who explains what the spirit/entity herself is not able to explain about her mental turmoil.

"The one you wanted, the one who in her past lifetime was known as one with mental illness, is here. Enter this one's name as Edna."

My earth plane problems came about because I had no control over my thoughts. This state of affairs gave me little of value to put into my being. My body tried to stabilize by eating what was good, but my spirit self entered into a battle over what in my world was good and what was not.

Let me explain. My mental state came about because I entered earth life without any plan or gentle help from those who could guide me. This lack of plan kept me searching to learn why I was on earth. But those who surrounded me in the earth plane did not know my plan either. Some thought I was strange, but they believed that I was OK. That was the problem. No one agreed on what was wrong with me.

Tenderness from my parents tended to present the good in my life. However, when they tried to get me to act in one way or another, I believed that down deep they hated me. Confusion was my master.

The days were too long, and the nights were unbelievably full of my fears. But there was no way to get help. My parents, whom I trusted when a child, teamed up with those whom I could not trust (those who examined me). Therefore, I no longer trusted my parents.

EPILOGUE

Those who wanted me to team up with doctors wanted me to become something I didn't want to become. The whole earth plane experience was frightening. Therefore, I entered myself to this plane by putting myself into a car and running the engine with a hose that brought the fumes to my body self. That way I slept my life away knowing I'd not awake.

Imagine my great surprise when I did awake in this plane with all the same unsorted thoughts. My mind turned inside out here just as it had in the earth plane.

I know I sound entirely mixed up, but that was the way I lived my lifetime in the earth plane. Yes, all mixed up. Very tender teammates greeted me here when I awoke on this plane, and they have tried to help me to sort out my mixed up thoughts. This is what they do now, and I team up with them the best I can.

No one has greeted me here except for these who guide me, for no one wants to be around a mixed up entity. The thought process I go through is not best teamed up with anyone. Others fear they may catch what I have, whatever it is.

Gentle presences surround me night and day to help me, and they tell me that I will soon sort things out here. But I think those are just words.

On the earth plane I never could sort out my life, and now here I cannot sort it out either. The reason, these gentle presences tell me, is that I cannot distinguish between the thought that gives me those things I want from the thought that gives me the open truth. Therefore, I wallow in between somewhere not knowing which thought is valuable to keep and which thought is merely picturing what I see or want or need.

Entirely new thoughts present themselves to me sometimes, and I am told I must hold these thoughts in my mind and work with them that I may become one with them. These thoughts enter the truth about who I am, for example. Then another shows me how to put one thought at a time into my mind and to distinguish between the open truth and the mere thought that brings me what I need or want.

This all sounds easy to you, perhaps. But I know it is not easy for me. The guides watch me closely and keep me within their group to prevent me from going back to earth life too soon. They tell me I would have the same state of affairs again if I return too soon. I do not want that. Too many people cried over me there, and I cried over myself in a way.

There is nothing else at present. The arms of these who bring their tenderness surround me now to keep me quiet, to keep me still, to help me to put myself into quiet energy where I can learn what I must learn.

With this last statement, Edna withdrew.
I asked the advanced spirit who brought me this disturbed entity what caused her mental illness. This is the reply.
"Entirely too much teaming up with earth-mind truth has brought this one into the gibberish that she now speaks. This entity got away from us to reunite with a body sooner than she should. She got into the body but could not stabilize there. Her truth is too weak; her tenderness is too shallow; her peace of mind is non-existent.
"During past lifetimes in the earth plane, this entity had put the earth truth above all other, and this truth caused her to have painful experiences. Therefore, this one equated her recent lifetime experience with the painful experiences of another lifetime. She cannot rid herself of those experiences to create a new lifetime experience.
"The only way this one can be new in mind and new in heart is to grow spiritually to the point where she is once again open to the God of the Universe. But now she is not even able to acknowledge her God self! This entity causes us much energy here, much work. This one will be taken to a place far from this plane while she gets acquainted once again with her true nature which is of God. We will not let her enter earth life again with this undernourished truth."

Nancy

17

When I read in my newspaper about the death of a recognized artist, I clipped the obituary. Here was an opportunity, I hoped, to learn what the next plane of life looked like. Surely this spirit, whose lifetime was devoted to art, could give a detailed description of the next plane of life. However, what I received was far different from what I expected.

"Tender thoughts enter when you call the name of Nancy," Love said. "This entity who was the artist you seek sends her good wishes to you, and she wants to know the reason for your seeking her."

I explained (by thought) that I was gathering material for a book about the experiences of various spirit entities concerning their recent lifetimes, their death experience and their ongoing lives.

Love answered, "This entity now positions herself at your own shoulder to write through you."

Tenderness rises within me now when I speak of this experience in what you call the next plane of life. The plane that appears to me to be the next plane of life is the earth plane, not this one. In my observation, the plane I am in is the home base for those who want to get to the point of re-entering the life process.

Better tenderness I have not known anywhere than I receive here. It is overwhelming me every way. The tenderness I speak of is not the kind that the earth plane furnishes us, but the kind that emanates through the cosmic universe where the planets meet. It is the kind of tenderness that only the God of the Universe has to give. Entering into this is a most pleasant experience, for it makes me want more and more. I may never be satisfied, but I hope I will finally open myself to enough tenderness to be totally eternalized as the one with pure tenderness in her being.

This tenderness never seems to go away; it abounds. It holds me within itself, opening itself to my being without reservation. I had hoped to enter into God's love while in the earth life. But the newness of spirit never seemed to take hold there. Tenderness here, however, invades my every thought to enter into God's Pure Tender Truth. This truth heals me, and it eternalizes what I want in my life.

Nothing in my earth experience teamed up with what was most beautiful or most satisfying because I needed tenderness. The need overwhelmed me and gave me no peace. But now I have peace, for I am receiving all the tenderness that I need.

To move to the point of this interview, I asked if she was an artist.

Yes, art was my entire life. It took my time, my thought, my everlasting good sense. But inside the reality of myself, I hid the utter tenderness that wanted to be expressed. That is where I thought I had to hide it so I would not let any other person know my longing.

But the longing wanted expression. It needed to be fulfilled. The part of me that hid things hid this terrible need for tenderness. But now thoughts come to me to be understood and to be teamed up with my being which is seeking to have itself renewed.

No one who knew me in the earth life would think this is I speaking to you because I hid my inner self not only to their eyes but to my eyes too. Now the hunger within me must be satisfied. That is why I explain it to you over and over. The truth within me must be entered into, and it is to be understood. No one, my guide tells me, teams up with those who will take one to higher planes until each unfilled need of the previous lifetime experience is met straightforwardly and with the thought of being understood. What I am doing now is getting the truth into my entity's focus; it is a growth process that I am going through.

As an artist, I knew she would be observant of details, and I was still trying to get that description I wanted. I asked her to describe the place where she was.

This appears to be a place where I reside at the present moment but not the place where I will eventually go. Entering through the ether to this place was rather vague, to tell the truth. The entire experience of coming here—dying, I suppose it was—was not at all clear to me. What a disappointment, eh? But eternal thought greeted me, and then we went to the matter at hand, my own present condition, how to move off the reception of earth energy and to get onto the higher vibration. This was step one.

The truth that came toward me came from within me, yes, but only because at last I had the ears to hear. Eternal music surrounds me too, but the truth pours through to me to bring my vibrations to an ever increasing energy level. That is why this entity that I am sends these thoughts about what I am doing. The present situation is what you—or anyone—might find yourself in, after all. That must be the purpose in writing this book, to know what it is like."

Once more I appealed to the artist in her. "What about sight? Will you say something about what we might see there?"

Sight is not what comes first. The first thing is the experience itself, not the sight. I have sight, but details are vague. I am not blind, I am told, but I have no way yet of attaining the kind of vision that will open this place to me. When I am here longer, perhaps, I may send my thoughts to you again to enter into the business of sight. The experience is all there is now, and it enters my being as perfectly planned. It is what I want most, the exhaustive tenderness that is given me. Teaming up with this tenderness is what I do now to take me to the next step in this plane of existence.

Giving up on getting a description, I asked, "Would there be any advice at this point in your experience that you would want to give those still in the earth plane?"

No. The experience will be different for each one because, I am told, each of us is different. One may need tenderness, like me. Another may need open truth on the matter of growth. The circumstances differ also, I'm told. The lifetime that I had was long—98 years. It had productivity, but it lacked tenderness. That is why my experience is unique. There is no advice; no. But you may give this epilogue to the book so that others may gain their own understanding from it.

"Thank you for contributing your story," I wrote. "The story is enlightening, and I will include it in the book." I asked if there was anything more she wanted to say.

Nothing more.

Since Nancy had suggested that she might be able to give me the description I wanted after she had received all the tenderness she needed, much later I asked for her again. Love said she was ready to give me the description I asked for.

EPILOGUE

Teaming up with what is here is not easy, my Truth Giver. Those who want to understand the picture I now paint on the canvas of this word processor must have open minds. Eternalize, if you will, our grand and glorious conceptions of what we each think heaven is, and then team that up with what you want this place to be. There! You enter a picture that will closely resemble what you will find in this plane!

No one here will give exactly the same picture. Eternalizations abound here—eternalizations of what is perfect, you understand. Then, because our thoughts enter into one or another of the variety of possibilities, our teamwork produces still another picture. Enter that into your pipe and smoke it!

Startled by the homely expression, I stopped to re-read the above paragraph. "You are saying, it seems to me," I began, "that everyone produces his own environment!"

That is the way it seems, yes. But there are those who group themselves into communities to have an enlarged picture. These make the optimum energy of the universe work within their communities by producing what is perfect according to the best thinking there. Then, within that community, the entity may produce a true individual picture.

Puzzled, I asked for some kind of example.

No entity who wants to be on his own will join the community, you see. But if an individual entity does join the community, then that entity must support the environment. Each entity has a responsibility in that overall picture. Each one enters, say, into the community where his or her spirit feels at home. The ones already there have entered into a project of making their community beautiful.

A new entity enters. He may say, "Oh, this would be much better if you would put a stand of redwood trees over there." But others say, "No. We have it perfected. You may, however, use the place given to you and put redwood trees on it, just so long as you take care of them and keep them beautiful."

No one may enter and change the overall picture of the broad view of landscape, but each may put whatever he or she wants on the space set aside for that one's creativity.

I interrupted. "What are you putting into your space?"

A teamwork of artists will aid me in putting my beautiful landscapes (painted in earth life) into the actual scene. The artist and the canvas is one kind of teaming up, but those who produce all that into the environment are another kind of artist, the sculptor. My own landscape will reflect what I consider lovely beyond compare, that which teams up with my being.

I asked if various kinds of landscapes sit side by side.

The landscape is hidden by high bushes, perhaps, or water borders it or some other compatible natural scene. Then the individual puts in a landscape just suited to that one. Mine, as you know, is the southwestern United States landscape where rock and sand combine, the teeming desert that reflects the multitude of colors, the wonderful aridity of the complex teaming up of what brings us into tender thoughts.

"So each person puts an individual landscape into this community?"

That is right. This sounds weird, perhaps, but when you see it, you know that the entities merely build what suits them. Then you see with great appreciation what is wonderfully perfect in this one's or another's eyes. No spirit is like another. Those who are here live according to the truth of their beings, and though those in communities agree on most things, there are differences. This is their entire truth here, projected for all to see.

I agreed that it all sounds very different from the earth plane. I asked if one person could insert a mountain, for example, and Nancy quickly responded.

This is possible, of course. But you must know how it looks. Is it rock? Is it lava construction? Is it the rounded hills of the eastern United States, or the high jagged mountains of the West? This entry must be well understood, or there will only be confusion, no beauty.

"What about color?"

Those who enter color keep the sky blue and the clouds white as they had on earth. But those who wish to make life team up with what they feel inside, sometimes put in harsh colors to reflect their states of mind. These entities team up with others who share viewpoints, and then their entire environment is that of the dark landscape, the threatening clouds, the lightning and thunder, the constant threat of harsh weather. These entities know no better, it seems. They have never teamed up with beauty.

I asked Nancy another question. "If you were talking to a person who is afraid of the next plane of life, what would you say?" I waited for an answer, and it exploded through my own mind and onto the word processor screen.

The truth! This plane is what you make it, obviously. That was true of earth plane too, but few understood this. The ones who wonder about this plane could team up with the truth while in earth life and get their new perspective into what this plane is, but the entities I knew hardly spoke of these matters.

If I could give them my word of advice, I would say, "Team up with those who enter the earth plane to help you to put your life into the noble and eternal endeavors. Then you will learn about truth which will sustain you there and bring you here safely."

"The beauty of earth is still entered into my mind, but I see now that the possibilities here overshadow even what I had there. This is what I would tell one who wondered if the next plane of life could possibly be as wonderful as earth life!

I asked if there was anything else she wanted to say.

Now I enter into my tenderness again. I wear it like a cloak of gold here, wear it to hold me in the mighty Entity who gives His Being to my use. This tenderness puts me into the teamwork that I do here with each entity who helps me along. The tenderness shields me when I have no knowledge, when I look backward, when I wonder if I can go forward, when I hold thoughts of weakness. The cloak of tenderness reminds me that I am indeed special, that I am wonderful, that I am the precious one who receives great gifts of this One known as the God of the Universe.

Various thoughts enter me all the time to tell me truth, to bring me joy. Golden tables abound with gifts, and I eternalize what I must in order to have the gifts put into use here. What a wonderful experience I am having, what a grand and glorious place!

Bret

18

One person pointed out to me that we spend most of our lives in our work place. Therefore, of what spiritual significance is that work, he wondered, and how might we approach our choice of work? An immediate response came from Love.

"Work is just one way to express your truth, whatever it is. Some may express earth truth, and they will work hard and long. Others will express God truth, and they will work with the ease of perfect understanding, perfect accomplishment.

"The idea that your choice of work is teamed up with the God of the Universe is an erroneous thought. The work you choose may give great satisfaction to your being, or it may not. The worth of your work is based on how well you use truth in accomplishing it, not how valuable the job is to human kind. Therefore, to entertain any idea that one job is worth more than another is absurd.

"The idea that the harder you work, the more valuable you are as a person is not true either. The one who gives his life to his work, no matter what that work is, is not entering into a balanced lifetime. The eternal truth to take into account here is that your work is one expression of your truth, not the total expression of your being.

"We now enter together, the one who will give you his work story and I, to present the God truth of work. The one who tells his story is called Bret."

Whenever I brought my being into quiet meditation, I received perfect eternal truth that indicated to me, even when I was very young, that I had important work to do. The way I teamed up with this thought was to open myself to perfection—to the God way of doing things. The eternal truth stood there to be used, not to be wasted, and the openness with which I received it made its purpose clear.

71

The truth I came to express concerned the eternalization (projection) of truth into the ether or substance that we may use while in earth plane. This substance became earth material. Though this may seem strange to some, there will be readers who have enacted this very truth in their own lives.

The need of education became apparent right at the outset of my plan to put truth into earth plane. Entering earth truth said that I had no money, no opportunities, no hope of entering higher education. But the God truth said to eternalize the matter, and I did. That which I projected into the ether substance that surrounds the earth plane went into action on my behalf, and I became a student with good resources.

Yes, I worked very hard. Time went very fast, however. The truth that I kept on applying said to do this or to do that to enable my brain to learn, and I followed through. The truth worked on my behalf, and I entered into the accomplishment of my goal—an education—in a shorter time than I expected. The reason I could do this thing without great turmoil and without great agony of mind or body was that I used truth to help me. When the truth works its way, the path is made easy!

The work I then went into held my interest all my days. The time spent in this work was well spent, happy and productive time. The truth that I made use of helped me daily to achieve goals that I set. Truth helped me to get along with those with whom I worked. The truth that I came to express did so in the way I worked, not in the content of it. I did not preach or become a person who gave philanthropically. I endeavored to put the entire truth into practice in my work methods, and in my interacting with others. The truth was my life, not the work itself.

So that you may understand this thing, I will tell you of a situation that developed when I was about half way through my life experience. The one who was my boss thought I had things too easy. He wanted me to hurt at my work as he hurt. Therefore, he began to make life very hard for me.

There was a time period when I focused on this person, held him up to my thoughts even when I went home to those I loved. This seeming enemy began to dominate my life, my understanding, and he even thwarted my getting of truth. My health began to fail, my body suffered greatly, and I wanted release from what I thought was the enemy.

Then, meditating clearly for the first time in months, I saw the supposed enemy for what he was—the uncertain and perturbed individual who had no peace of mind, no eternal truth operating in his life. Poor pathetic person!

With this understanding came the way to work with this person, the way to probe beneath the facade he presented, and the way to give my own truth an opportunity to manifest in his environment. This truth I opened to gave me the release I needed from what my wrong perceptions had held me to. Then I brought my eternal truth into play, and it had its way in the situation. The enemy became neutralized, and I was freed to live and work.

The only way to enjoy work in the earth plane is to open yourself to God truth and make no room for earth truth. Then opportunities will abound in the work place and in the periphery of your work where you will have the energy to take on interesting tasks.

What else is there to add? What else could be more clear?

Thelma

19

Is there some spirit entity who would be willing to discuss a past lifetime which ended in the throes of alcoholism?
"The one who willingly enters now wants to explain why alcohol puts its hold onto the body of the susceptible. This one wants to explain why a person submits to this degrading experience and why no plan of tender truth was worked out. The entity who enters wants you to put the name of Thelma on this writing."
Quickly a second spirit took over.

Nothing in my past lifetime experience ended as it was supposed to. The plan I took into life discouraged the very truth I thought to express. You see, my plan held God truth, but I had no thought of expressing it to anyone. When great truth entered my being, I experienced inspiration. For awhile I worked furiously with this truth in mind. But then it faded because I did not plan how to put it into my life.

Here is how it works: Each entity comes to earth to use the truth that makes up the lifetime plan. No one has exactly the same plan because each of us is different. But the entity that I was turned herself to optimum energy only long enough to tune in to God-mind. Then I turned away again to the truth of mankind that announced the hopelessness of all creation.

The good truth entered just to exasperate me, just to turn me into one who hated what I understood of this earth and its people. "How could people be the way they are?" I thought. "What is this world coming to?" I said to my spirit self. My thoughts never were positive; they had only the worst of earth-mind truth in them. That is why I finally gave in to depression.

My lifetime consisted of this up and down experience of the wonderful truth followed by the "facts" which I believed in, "facts" that emptied themselves upon my spirit self to extinguish what was left of God thought.

"I cannot stand this!" I cried out. "God enters only to die of people's disinterest!"

The way out of my misery was the putrid belief that if I might subdue my body, I could rise above what I perceived to be intolerable. Therefore, my basic idea of subduing what was physical began and ended with discouragement. The terrible truth I made my own was that if I drank enough of the worldly spirits, I would rise above what is of earth into what was truly of God.

The basic idea of being one with God was within my being as it is within you, too. We all want to become one with God because it is written in the law. That desire was behind my wrong turn. But taking the turn I did, I hastened my inability to wrest anything of value from my lifetime experience. I wasted my life! The truth manifested to wring its hands at my misunderstanding. But I made it impossible, finally, to let any truth at all emerge.

The way I died, I think, was in the throes of delirium tremens. The way, however, is now unimportant, and I have no real memory of it. For those who had to stand by to see it happen, however, it must have been a horror.

Now I wrest what is valuable from my mistakes. Now I learn my lessons and make a new plan which will go with me when I re-enter a life experience. The truth eternalized within me now is to express what God-mind truth I understand, no matter what others do. What others do is not my concern! The matter of how to express my own truth is what I must be concerned with. In that way I will enter into a life experience that is not wasted. The main concern of any lifetime experience is to hold to the truth no matter what enters as the challenge. The truth held onto and expressed—that is the purpose. That one truth is what I now put into my new plan.

Entities gather around me now, those who had the same misuse of their lives that I had. They want me to add something here about their thoughts on alcoholism. The entire opinion seems to be that the problem of their drinking is centered in the opinions they held, such as thoughts of hopelessness. The opinion here is that though the body becomes saturated with alcohol to the point where it cries out for it, the initial thinking is at fault, not the body self.

There is one here who insists that the body enters into this scheme of things, but this one says that the thoughts that enter with God truth can bring such a body to wholeness. Therefore, though the body may have certain impulses from past physical expressions, perhaps, the entering truth can overcome these.

"Do you mean," I asked, "that if you were an alcoholic in a past life, you might bring that craving into a new bodily expression?"

The one who brings this idea thinks so. Those surrounding me do not all agree. Perhaps we express the truth only for ourselves, and that is why we disagree. The decision of putting the body to sleep in order to rise above what is of the earth is a common denominator, however. We all agree on that. The part where we disagree is on the body itself, if it—on its own—has thoughts of desiring alcohol.

We who are here know, however, that the way to nowhere as far as earth life is concerned is to put the body to sleep by artificial means—alcohol, other drugs, sleeping tablets. Even the final act of killing the body outright is no way to overcome the world.

The eternalization we each have about our lives is very much alike. Each of us wants to go back to the earth plane with the truth that the only way to cope with the world is to do what we each came to do—express whatever God truth we brought along as well as whatever truth we receive from God while we are in the earth plane. We must ignore the others who bring despondency; ignore those who would make us believe no truth can conquer the pending travails of the world. We are not responsible for others. We are only responsible for ourselves!

Believe in our mission. Believe that the entire problem of alcoholism is that the individual has become lost within the universal truth and the earth-mind which negates all the good he perceives.

"In Alcoholics Anonymous," I said, "part of the plan to help members recover is for them to help others like themselves. Don't they, then, become responsible for others?" The response was emphatic.

No! They may help, but if the one they try to help decides to drink anyway, are they to hold themselves responsible? The idea of helping is, we think, good. But to hold ourselves responsible if what we do does not work is to fall again into the old thought pattern that made us alcoholics.

Our combined thoughts here make the statement that we hold no fear of returning to earth life. We go forth assured that we know how to meet whatever befalls. Those who had alcoholism will team up with advanced spirits in this plane who will help us in our lifetime experience to become whatever it is we go to become.

The way to health is by way of thought. We who were alcoholic team up with thoughts of wholeness, of perfection, of the greatness which is of God. Then we depend on these here in this plane who will help us when we return to the earth plane. They will team up with us to bring us into the God-mind connection where we will each receive the Pure Truth we need to live successful lives.

Those who may read this in the earth plane—those who are now alcoholics—may open themselves now to this plane where much help is available. The way to get into the eternalization of the recovered alcoholic is to know the Pure Truth that enters from God-mind to your own mind by way of the open channel. Turn yourself toward the help of the Brothers, those who reach out to you in great tenderness. They work the eternalization with you, the eternalization of the beings who enter sobriety to become their full potential.

Ben

20

Some people are very sure of a place they call "heaven." They have what their church calls "salvation," and their ideas on what the next life will be like are very firm. How do their ideas mesh with the reality of the next plane?

"Those who have firm ideas on the subject of this next plane of life team up with what the church teaches, but they do not team up at all with reality. The one who approaches now is one who entered this plane steeped in the church-taught truth that each person stands at the judgment seat. Then, if this one is 'saved,' the entity goes forward into paradise.

"To wrest this thinking from the reader's mind, we introduce Ben, the one who entered here with his own ideas of what he must find, who must greet him, and how he must be treated. To get the open truth on this matter, we call on Ben to give his own story.

Now I have entered into peace within myself about this second plane of life, but when I first arrived, I was overwhelmed by disappointment. I had these ideas that the ministers taught in my church. They talked of streets paved with gold, the waiting arms of Jesus, the place where the "saved" may assuredly enter. But I could not find what I expected.

I had no fear of death because I knew I was saved. I had acknowledged that I was a sinner, that I wanted to confess my sins and that I wanted salvation. I gave my heart to Jesus as best I could, not ever having seen Jesus myself. But yet I loved what I knew of this Savior. Therefore, I began to live my life according to what Jesus would do in my place. Well, that pattern worked well for a time. I held to it the best I could, but when I failed, in great remorse I again confessed my sinfulness and found release in the conviction that I was forgiven.

Then I had an awesome event enter into my life. My work had dangerous side effects. I became ill—the body self of me—due to the substances I worked with. I accepted the potential deadly effects because I knew I was saved. My wife and I talked with the minister, and the church and the minister prayed for me—for my health, I suppose. No one ever said exactly what they were praying for. I assumed they prayed for me to get well.

Inside my being, however, I did not want to get well. I was finished with earth life as I understood it, and I thought the next plane of life would be preferable. The minister and I talked about heaven, about hell, about the "most High God" who would undoubtedly have a place for me there. I quivered with nervousness, for I could not really imagine God other than a mighty giant.

I held to my understanding of Jesus, however. I held to that image right through death and right into this plane of life. But there the image faded. I found a spirit entity, all right, but he did not look like the pictures I had seen in the Bible or upon the windows of the church. Where was the white robe, the burnished gold hair, the tender blue eyes, the compassionate look?

I was disappointed. There's no other way to put it. I refused the guide's offers to help and began, on my own, to seek those who could explain to me what I could not understand.

It occurred to me that I had come to hell. Yes, I actually thought that since there was no street of gold, no singing choirs to greet me, no outstretched arms of either Jesus or God, that perhaps I was in hell. Then I began to think I must be in some inbetween place like Catholics believe. I ran wildly from one place to another and peeked into the groups that clustered here and there, but I found no comfort, no place for me. The guide trailed me patiently, smiling tenderly.

There is no use in recounting the whole thing to you. It is very repetitious, for I went again and again to the various clusters in the hope of recognizing someone I knew. But no one approached. Then I just gave up. The guide who followed me said later that he carried me to a temple where I slept and then awoke slowly to the sounds of gentle music and words of truth. I lay there a long time, he tells me, until I understood that this plane of life was not what I had expected at all. What I had expected was not possible, for I projected a place created by earth-mind, not a place created by God-mind.

Nothing that I eternalized (projected mentally) worked in this plane because I did not understand God truth. I thought I had believed in a mighty God, but my understanding of God was weak indeed! The way to eternalize in this plane is to work with God principles. Otherwise, one can do nothing to bring good into being.

Remember, I had no fears of death, no projections of judgment either because I knew I was saved. Therefore, I did not project fears. But I could not project the kind of heaven I expected because this concept was not in line with God truth. Do you understand?

I affirmed that I understood. Then I asked, "What is the difference between the principles you used and God principles?" I sensed a wryness in his tone, a subtle change in his vibrations.

The truth I entered into while in the earth life had little that was of God truth. That must surprise you. But I held a narrow thought of the "few that would be saved." God's principles team up with what is most generous, not with the narrow view that excludes anyone. My truth in my earth life was based on fear, partially. I feared going to hell. I feared not meeting God. I feared going down the wrong path in earth life and becoming entangled with wrong ways.

I wanted the certainty of salvation. I wanted to know that I would go to heaven. There are many views of how to accomplish these aims in earth life, and the choice was difficult. But because I met several people who were certain their church had the ideas down correctly, I joined with them.

What I did was to close my mind, my spirit self, to the adventure of talking with God-mind or walking a unique path that was mine to walk. I chose, instead, the path of Jesus and tried to make myself in his image—an impossibility. I did not try to form a concept of God on my own because I thought that would be dangerous. Therefore, whatever was told me, that was what I tucked away in my mind.

The God of the Universe—that powerful tender presence that pours truth to each of us—was unknown to me.

Momentarily the message stopped. I waited. Finally, he continued with slow deliberation.

The way to get on track is to bring new truth into my mind until I can stand without crutches. My best understanding is only now beginning to enter my being. I see with clarity the why's of my mistakes, and I see with clarity my good intentions. Now I want to be a partner with what is truly God. That is my own decision after hearing the truth, after working with my understanding guide, after searching this plane for the heaven that I thought existed and then entering into disappointment.

The message had become so slow that I interrupted to ask questions. First, I asked, "Did you ever find hell?"

There is no "hell" in the way I thought of it. The way the truth works, the principle of God, is that when I accept that God is to be understood as open ended, as truly all good, all understanding, then how can I expect to find a "hell?" God IS what He IS—total goodness. God IS the totality of power, and there is NO OTHER GOD BESIDE HIM. Therefore, where is that evil entity who welcomes us into hell? I cannot find any such entity or any such place.

My second question was, "Have you met Jesus?"

There is a group of advanced ones here who are the Brotherhood who work with those in the earth plane. The guide who helps me has explained them to me. The one they call the Brother of Brothers is that Jesus, but he is not what I expected. No, he is not the great individual who selects which will be saved, which believed on him, not the one who opened the only truth that is upon those who have ears to hear. No, the Jesus I know of here is working to bring each spirit to the God of the Universe, not to himself. I had thought in my earth life that to go to Jesus was the same as going to God, but the Jesus here says "not so."

"One final question," I said. "What would you say to those you cared for in the earth life if you could talk to them?" His reply was emphatic.

I can talk to them. I try to reason with them, but I meet great resistance. The minister I went to in the earth plane hears me every now and then. He shakes his head and prays to be free of what he thinks are "evil thoughts" that try to take him from God. The guide I have says that there are better ways to project God-mind truth than by trying to communicate with them. But as yet I have not learned what these ways are.

I know a tenderness here that I never knew before. This tenderness flows through me and is a gift from God. This tenderness is what I need to become one with, what I need most in my being. It, the tenderness, will not condemn people, it will not put my judgment upon them, it will not hope for a personal heaven where I and only a few others will be in

God's grace. No, the tender truth of God is pouring over me now, and my mind is absorbing it. That is all I need to have right now.

In response to my silent question asking if he wanted to say more, he gave me a definite "No."

Each one who enters here must find his own way. I cannot give it to them. But were I to understand in my earth life what I understand now, I would have put myself into the outpouring of God's gifts that I might have lived my life with the openness of one who is assured of his relationship with God, not one who must search, worry, beg, weep, be teamed up with what others say. That is all I can tell you right now, and I welcome your including it in the book.

Peter
21

I asked to speak to someone who has used fasting and/or other physical denial as a means to spiritual development.

"The person who enters now to reflect upon this question determined his own spiritual development on earth by entering into the denial you speak of. This one opened himself to new growth by emptying himself of all physical interest. Entering now to speak to you on this matter is the one we like to call Peter—the Entity Who Teams Up With Pure Truth. (This was the second spirit named Peter who gave his story for this book.)

"Those who came to him to be taught epitomized his spirituality by calling him 'the one who could walk on water.' No one else from this plane can enter to give you this sort of writing because the advanced ones who enter higher planes team up with the work of that plane, not this one. Now here is Peter who gives his own version of what self denial means to the spirit."

My name is Peter, the entity of Eternal Truth. I have been here in this place where the entities rest between lives to ready myself for another plunge back to earth life. Every time I return I try to eternalize some new truth that will open me to higher vibrations and which will help advance earth-mind truth.

Now I would like to speak to the readers who question about the spiritual development they might create in the earth lifetime by putting their physical selves into secondary importance.

No one who enters life on earth can completely omit concern over the body, for it is the vehicle for the expression of truth. By omitting concern, the body may weaken and thereby not serve either you or any other entity who might take over, not even the world itself. Therefore, give the body what is due the body to keep it well and healthy. That is the necessary part that all spirit entities must know.

No entity who takes a body may neglect it through eternalizing only the spirit! Becoming one with truth is not the only goal of each entity. Truth must be expressed in the lifetime experience. That's the way the principle works. No amount of self-denial will advance the spirit if the spirit denies this fundamental principle. The body and the world itself must reflect the truth you take unto yourself. By way of your own demonstration of truth, others will enter into it also."

I asked Peter if he practiced self-denial in his last lifetime.

The entity that I was intended only to serve the spirit. I opened myself to every thought of how my body might be banished from my thinking in order to enter into great spirituality. That plan did not work for me. No one, in fact, can banish the body! At least not until the spirit leaves the body and comes here.

I went too far with the banishment of the physical, but in a new lifetime I hope to strike a balance. My plan now is to reach a goal of being the truth in expression, and it includes how to use this spirit growth in the physical domain in which I live.

The new lifetime plan I work with now is to concentrate on God truth and how to demonstrate it before mankind. Those who see will understand where the good comes from, and they will themselves be enriched. The earth-mind truth will record my attainments, and others may thereby know the strength of Pure Truth.

No, I will not go to excess in bringing comfort to my body. I will not give the body what is too rich, what is too intoxicating, what will put it into jeopardy. The plan is that I, in this next lifetime, will have nourishment to sustain the body and help it to express my plan.

Thinking that Peter may have a worthwhile plan for bodily health, I asked if he could tell us about it that we might use it too.

No. The body that I find myself in will be unique, and the way it must be cared for depends on what develops there. The Brotherhood of God here on this plane will be here to enter their help when I need it, to give me counsel, to bring me into Pure Truth. In this way I will not depend only upon the knowledge I now have stored within me.

"Do you have any advice," I asked, "for people who fast and otherwise try to bring their bodies into submission to the spirit?" I waited only a moment for the answer.

No. The presumption in your question is that I have the answers that will open truth to everyone, and of course that is not possible. All must find the truth of God that applies to their own beings. They must also give that truth only unto themselves, not to others. So, eternalize what is right for you within your own being, but think not to turn another toward your own truth. Each entity eternalizes what is right only for the one.

The entity that I am now is not the same one who expressed in his last lifetime experience. Whatever you in the earth plane may think now, I tell you that when you come here and work through your identity, you are never just the one who lived in the past lifetime. That one has merged into the one you really are—the one who entered into many lifetimes. Only the truth remains, you see, the truth which is your entire being—yes, the identity.

Thomas

22

A person with whom I shared these epilogues suggested I seek an interview with one who had been homosexual in the recent lifetime experience. Unhesitatingly, Love brought me "tenderness expressed as Thomas."

"The one who now approaches says that he was one of those who entered life without plan or without good truth. Better truth is worked out now, however. With this in mind, Thomas enters to bring you his thoughts on why he was not content to be what the growth plan laid out before him."

New understanding shows me what my entire lifetime experience was about. I rejected what my parents gave me— my physical entity which was a boy's body. The plight I thought I had was that in reality I was not male, but rather, female. This thought possessed me night and day when it finally took hold of me.

"Why?" I cried out. "What is the justice of having a body I do not want?" The more I lamented the condition, the worse it became. I found my own body intolerable. This kind of thought is not conducive to spirituality growing within the body, is it? My consuming thought became physical, not spiritual.

Then, with desperate hope, I teamed up with other males who were also dissatisfied with their sexuality. We had tenderness for one another, and we gave satisfaction to our bodies. But still there was discontent! Nothing I did opened the way to perfect understanding of myself. But nevertheless, in some ways I grew less discontented.

No one can perfectly understand what I say—not this writer, certainly, or anyone who has never experienced such discontent with his body. Even now I remember it with emotion! Even now I enter a plea for understanding by those who never hated their own bodies, never had a thought of being other than what their bodies indicate.

This particular aspect of homosexuality focuses on those who begin new lives in the earth plane without working through their plan. Those of us here who work together to understand our peculiar energy, team up with what is unusual in the way of explanation, perhaps. The way we think it happens, this discontent, is that we hated our sexuality in past lifetimes.

I hated males when I lived before, you see. They oppressed me, who was female then. They treated me as property. They used me. The hate goes very deep even now.

The way to free myself of this hate is to realize that it is hate itself that binds me to the male body. The only way I can empty out this hate is to become the male who enacts the goodness of God toward women, toward all humanity. This, then, is my own explanation for the entire episode I lived through in my last lifetime.

I asked if Thomas had a guide who helped him sort through his problems.

The guide who met me here when I died taught me that each one must examine past lives to find answers to why the past lifetime was or was not lived successfully. I have been here a long time, for there are many, many lifetimes to go through and examine. But what emerges for me is this pattern of hate for the male person throughout my long series of lifetimes. The entity that I was in my past lifetimes turned against what was male. Therefore, when I went to earth life (last time) as a male, the whole roof caved in.

Others here tell of similar happenings, but not all stories of homosexuals are the same, of course. There is another here who speaks of hate for the male because in the past lifetime he was abused by one male who enacted the role of the husband. This husband entered again into the most recent lifetime as the brother. This entity hated his brother without reason, without cause. And along with the hate came his turning against all that was male.

The whole business of the lifetime experience rests on the matter of being the God self one wants to be. This God self is neither male nor female, neither man nor woman. Therefore, if I put my God self into good order, it will not matter what body form I take. The form is immaterial in the entire sense of spirit growth.

I asked Thomas if he had any advice for homosexuals in the earth plane.

No. Each person, homosexual or heterosexual, teams up with whatever truth that is brought with that spirit to the earth life. If the person brings the truth that God is the Source, God is the Entire Truth, then the growth plan will enact whether or not that one enters willingly into the male or female body. The entity must work out for himself the truth of his being, not I.

"Then you are saying," I interrupted, "that everyone can work out his growth plan whether or not he is homosexual?" Thomas answered quickly.

That is true. Homosexuality can be overriding in life, or it can be quietly teamed up with gentle emotions. In my own case, it was overriding because I had hate as the basis of it.

I asked if Thomas believed that homosexuals are punished by God because of the lives they live. His response was emphatic.

No. God does not punish! Punishment comes only from within. Those in earth life, however, take it upon themselves to give punishment, of course.

I asked about disease—AIDS, for example.

Entities who have this disease must work through it as any entities must work through disease. This disease is no different in its growth than any other. The only truth to overwhelm AIDS is the truth which enters us as God Himself who brings wholeness simply because He is that Wholeness. That is the way to team up with the truth.

"The Bible mentions homosexuality as unrighteousness. (I Corinthians, 6:9) Will you comment on this?"

Unrighteousness is mentioned, but the judgment that is given is not from God, but from men. The unrighteous were condemned by those who wanted to regulate society by warning people that their thoughts were leading them away from God. Therefore, those who study this part know that their petty thoughts, their petty feelings may lead them into dangerous waters.

No, the entity that I was (in my past lifetime), did not believe that God turned from him. I knew what it was to love, and I realized that God's tenderness for me surpassed anything that I manifested toward others. Therefore, no entity could convince me that I was condemned. The entity that

91

EPILOGUE

I am now, however, knows that my lifetime was unproductive because it was the result of hate. No amount of entering tenderness ever caused me to forgive what was male. There is the basic problem, the hate!

"Is there anything else you wish to add?" I asked.

Nothing. I now understand the lessons of my past lifetime in the light of the perspective of this plane and the entering truth of God.

Natural Disasters

23

Natural disasters such as earthquakes, hurricanes, tornados, floods and the like are often referred to as acts of God. I asked Love if someone there could comment on these occurrences and explain what happens to spirits who depart their bodies in such large numbers.

"New truth must be given here to those readers who may believe that God orders these cataclysmic events on the planet earth," Love began. "The truth enters through God-mind, not my own mind, for only God will put the matter straight. Therefore, open your minds to this explanation which we seek. Open the channel to that truth of truths that through the ages has entered itself to mankind when the question is put and the listening ear is given."

Here is the truth Love promised. "The 'disasters' that you name only reflect the earth in its turmoil, the earth trying to right itself to produce the truth of purity. When the earth shakes, when the earth belches forth its steam, when the water runs through new channels to overwhelm the earth, those who stand in the way must place themselves in the entire truth of tender teamwork.

"By 'teamwork,' the term that denotes the God-mind connection between that which is of God and that which resides within the body, we mean to say that only this oneness will sustain those who get into the midst of turmoil. People need not depart their bodies in such numbers; teamwork opens them to better avenues of escape, better ways of protecting those bodies. Those who tune in to God-mind truth stand ready to avoid this turmoil that enters the earth because of the earth's need to try to overcome its travail. Those who turn to God-mind, those who overcome the earth truth that denies the power of God, those who open their minds to what is absolutely true will overcome the world in physical ways as well as in spiritual matters. They are one—the mind and the body—when the entity teams up with God-mind to learn truth.

"No earth turmoil will take lives unless those who believe in the ravages of turmoil accept those ravages. Those who want no part of earth-mind truth will heed the warnings, heed the escape routes,

93

heed the voices that proclaim the way to safety. Yes, the way to safety is made clear to those who tune in to God truth, who open their minds to those who will help them through the growth periods that earth must exhibit.

"Those who turn to the earth-mind truth, however, those who know no other way, will not even know of the warnings that come to them, nor will they team up with possible protection. Earth-mind truth reflects what people have come to accept because they believe they are without power. They understand nothing of teamwork with the God of the Universe. They understand nothing of the possibilities because they have named the disasters, as they call them, 'acts of God.'

"The one who enters now eternalizes his earth experience that he might express as clearly as possible what occurred there. This entity teamed up with the idea that God was in charge of the planet earth to the extent of thinking He sent not only the awful events called 'acts of God,' but that He also sent the diseases that plague mankind, that he snatched people to His own Being whenever the fancy struck. Therefore, death, disease, and all natural occurrences were ascribed to the God whom this one invented, not the God of the Universe Who opens Himself to each one."

The day I entered this plane of life is clearly in mind now. The time of day was early Tuesday morning, and it was hot and muggy. Those who rose from their beds hurried to their work places, and I hurried along with them. The eternal truth of the planet, I learned later, is that it must stir up its resources periodically in order to create better environment. It has taken me quite a long while to understand this. But that day in question I had no thoughts of the earth nor of the God I then knew. I hurried along toward my work place teamed up with the purpose of earning money.

The earth rumbled, and I, who had heard the ominous rumble when I was a child, fell to my knees and implored God to save me. That was the way I acted then, the way I understood the God I knew. I saw God as the monster who created this rumble, the One Who would open the earth and bury me in it. Therefore, I thought only to appease this monster, to beg Him to stop, to enter into great groveling at His feet. Those around me did the same, but in the distance I heard one cry out, 'Tender God, I am running to the safe place.' I looked up but did not follow.

"Fool!" I thought. "What is he doing?" He turned and cried out to us to follow him, for he knew where to go to be safe. But I did not see anyone go. He picked up one small child, but his mother dragged him back to her bosom. Then the man turned quickly and ran. The rest of us waited to receive God's judgment, which is what we thought the earthquake was.

Buildings fell; the earth opened up; screams peeled into the air along with the dust that billowed gently up and over the whole scene. That I died is certain, but I do not actually remember it. The dying part just happened, but I did not know whereof it came.

The next thing I became aware of was standing there looking at the scene. The man who cried out to God and ran like the wind was weeping as he looked back. He began pulling others free from the rubble. The truth that had sustained him now led him to help others the best he could.

Around me stood thousands of spirits looking at the scene before us, looking in disbelief, in horror, for we thought ourselves still part of it all. Then the music began, and around us, through us, the music that teamed up with us overcame our horror. We saw clearly that we were now among the teammates who had left bodies behind. But when we saw that we were whole, that we were alive, we began to reflect our understanding. Then one by one I saw the spirits rise with the guide who came to help them. The scene below us faded, and we turned our eyes to the new life, to those who were ready to lead us forth into new experiences.

Nothing more came through to amplify the scene, and relieved, I ended the transmission.

Frances

24

Frances was born with an oxygen-deprived brain. Her physical existence depended completely on others. She could not move about nor feed herself. Her parents kept her at home with them for most of her life and tried to help her develop whatever resources she had. She died in her middle teens. When I asked about her ongoing spirit, Love said she was frolicking about and running because she was finally free. He said she would talk with me later.

What a wonderful image came to mind of her bright spirit running and skipping, enjoying the movement, the freedom. I waited a couple of days, and then I inquired if Frances was ready to communicate.

"The one you now open yourself to is not the one you saw in the body that had no way of expressing. The spirit of this one teams up with the truth and a vigorous expression of it. Her spirit is now ready to team up with you to bring you her own message."

Team up with my energy that enters this communication. The energy that I am is now opening to you who is ready to hear what I have to say. The new truth pours in to me and is welcomed by this spirit of mine. How hungry I am for truth! That which I heard in my lifetime teamed up mostly with the earth that gave me my body. The earth that brought my body had no way to improve it, no way to help its condition, so why heed what the earth-mind truth had to say to me?

That which I expressed in the lifetime just past was very little by earth standards, but within that poorly constructed brain I entered into my own understanding of truth that I brought with me. Each day I sent my thoughts outward, but there was no response from those who sent their own strong thoughts to me. They believed, you see, that I was that body, that brain, that outgenerated truth.

No such word as "outgenerated" appears in my dictionary, so I struck the question mark key several times.

I mean the kind of truth that said, "She will never be any different." Those who eternalized my condition helped cement it. But there are ways to open the so-called impossible cases when people know the truth.

My own truth came to me from God-mind, and I tried to work with it. That was my goal, to express the truth I knew. The way I worked, however, was to present the truth to my parents, to my teammates whoever they were. They, however, did not heed what I sent forth. Therefore, I remained as I was. The mistake I made was in not teaming up with the God of the Universe to undo the terrible thing that the earth truth had done. Work with the Teammate of Teammates would have brought me into better expression.

I thought I was to send the truth to those who seemed to me to be powerful. Now I see they were not powerful. They were weakened by the earth truth. The open manner in which I now embrace this understanding brings me the message that I must understand—that my parents could not help me because they knew no way. They relied on what they knew, not on the truth that poured in from God. But what I say is no reflection upon their beings, and I heap no anger upon them. No! I am glad just to be released so that I may go on with a brighter life experience.

Today I am reviewing my life. Tenderness was present for me, joy at each little tiny progress I made came through to me and stays with me now. Those who wished I would die, and there were many who thought I had come to hurt my family, team up now with better attitudes. They did not want to wish me dead, but they wanted my family's lives to be more normal. The way I view this is with understanding.

Nothing that enters my being now is filled with despair or with the feeling of missed opportunities. That lifetime was what it was, and before long I will probably re-enter the world to again try my hand at expressing truth.

My teammate, my guide, says that I am not near ready for that departure, and I know that spirit is right. I need much more in the way of generous play, and I want much more understanding of who I am before I again enter the body of a baby. The thought of confinement in a body right now is not what I want.

I stopped to ask this bright, energetic spirit what she would tell her parents today if she could get the message to them.

I would tell them not to be into any remorse or into any wonderment about where God is in this expression of my life. God IS. God eternalizes my good. The lifetime that I lived was not God truth in expression; God wanted me to have the truth of my being and bring it forth, but I could not. God enters with what He Is, with goodness, with wholeness, with perfection. That I did not express God is not the fault of God, after all. The responsibility for bringing forth what is of God lies within our individual spirits. They may not like these words and may like their implications even less because my parents team up with their own philosophies, their own understandings. But nevertheless, those are the things I would say to them if it were possible.

Now I go forth into this plane of life enjoying myself to the utmost. That is my sole purpose right now—to enter into great enthusiasm for this life. Now goodbye, Truth-Giver. My being longs to fly, to soar, to eternalize the high reaches of space.

Penny
25

Newspapers across the nation report an alarming number of suicides among teenagers. One school principal calls suicide an "epidemic" in his high school, and he said that mass counseling had been initiated to prevent any more young people from trying to take their lives. Two students were found in time to save them. Three others died. I asked Love for one of these young people who could explain why suicide seemed necessary.

Love brought me the one I asked for by saying, "Here she is."

I received a message of anger, mistrust and hopelessness. She said, among other things, that "I found no answers. That is why I emptied the bottle of pills into myself." Since her death, she had been visiting familiar places in the earth plane, she said, and she heard others trying to work through her death and the deaths of the other two teenagers. Speaking emphatically and with contempt, she told me there is nothing valuable in life for anyone, "and they either have to adjust to the emptiness or do what I did."

She insisted that even in the next plane of life she found nothing of value. "This place is the pits," she declared.

She accused me of calling her just to satisfy my curiosity. However, she insisted on knowing how I called her. I tried to explain. She responded, "This seems like rot to me." I was stung, I'm sorry to say, and I tried to enhance my reputation by explaining my noble purpose in writing this book. But she would have none of it.

"Good-bye, Truth-giver," she said. "The truth you write eternalizes within your soul, but I know it for what it is, the wrong truth. Trust the truth you see in the lifetime experience, that's what I say. There will be those here, I understand, who know what I mean. They will enter my space before long, and I will have those around me who think as I do. That is good enough for me."

Her words jarred my thoughts. I sat at my word processor for a long time re-reading her message. Then came a postscript from an advanced spirit in the Brotherhood of God. This message assured me that the spirit who spoke to me would eventually listen to her guide. "Do not think we give up on this one. We let her rave and rant while she settles down to listen. Then we can talk with her— by thought, of course."

Later, as I was organizing the book, I looked again at this downbeat message. My fingers were on the keys when one of the Brothers inserted this message: "The Brotherhood wants you to take the message again from this young one who opened herself to new life here in this plane. Give this one a new interview, for she has much of value to add."

Immediately she began.

Call me Penny because I am the coin of least value. The one you now ask for is here with new thoughts on the matter of entering this plane of tender truth. Put down what I say here because it may help some other teenager to sort out his lifetime.

The tenderness that has come into my life on this plane has made me enter into the full teamwork here. When I first arrived, entering with the truth of earth, none of the new God truth made sense to me. I put down whatever came to me of truth because I had never heard of it in earth life. A guide was there to help me when I arrived, but I sent this one away. Then I went with others to the place where God truth is not heeded, where everyone believes exactly alike. I soon understood I would have no life at all in that place. Therefore, I made a fast exit to find my guide still waiting to help me.

I explained what had happened to me inside the cluster of those who believed as I did that there is no truth here worth paying attention to. I wanted out, I told my guide. But out of pride, I stayed, never wanting to be wrong. The weird teammates I had there wanted me to enact my whole last lifetime for their entertainment. Enact my whole lifetime for entertainment! Can you beat that?

Never could I have believed anyone would be that gauche! They had no life other than going over one another's lifetimes, living it with them, having the miseries, the awfulness that led them all to do what I did—kill myself. But they had no ideas of anything better because they closed themselves in. That existence wasn't for me, I'll tell you! That's why I hastened out the door to the waiting presence of my guide.

102

Now every moment is teamed up with getting the real truth inside of me, the truth that enters me to make my lifetime become one of joy again. Nothing enters me now that is not the real truth. This is why I come to you now. The first time we met, I gave you the pits of myself. But now, at least, I give you the beginning of my upward thrust. The guide calls what I do "my upward thrust." Therefore, I can call it that, too. But saying it is a long way from understanding it.

Now my guide wants to give me this chance to write a better summation of myself. That may be a good idea because I see why I became hopeless in life. I see now why I killed my body. That is all very, very clear, but it is not good. The teaming up I did with the earth-mind truth convinced me there is nothing in life that can be counted on. My sadness was my total reality because I made my bed in the truth which entered into negativity, into hopelessness, into the terrible happenings I saw and read.

"Whatever can be done about the way the world is?" I'd say to myself. "What weighs me down?" I'd say this aloud whenever I was alone.

The world weighed me down because I bought the awful inferior truth that earth-mind taught. My truth then was, "Hate is all I see around me. Tenderness does not exist. Hopelessness is what everyone I know feels about life. They find no joy or happiness that I see! They give one another ugly words, guilt or anger. What's the use of growing up into a world like that?" Those were my thoughts!

The weight of it all lay upon my spirit. No one came into my life to present other opinions, other thoughts. Those in this plane who work with people who would end their own lives tried to reach through to me, my guide tells me. But the weight was too much. Therefore, thoughts came to mind that if I killed myself, then all my heaviness would disappear!

"Why, that must be the answer," I said to myself. The earth-mind truth, of course, revealed ways of doing this. Therefore, without much more thought, I simply ended my life. Then the other two, those guys who thought similar thoughts, they did the same. When we met here, guess what? Nothing was different! Our bodies were gone, of course, but not the problems, not the heaviness!

Then came the guides! The other two went off with their guides, but not me! I wasn't going to listen to some guide tell me I was wrong! That's where you found me the first time you called for me. My guide thinks if I now enter my new understanding that it may ring the genuine bell of recognition for some in earth life who may be thinking of suicide. I open the truth to them. That's all I have. The energy I spent on my grief in the earth plane could have been better spent in getting the truth of God-mind.

Yes, I could have gotten this great truth had I tried a simple method called eternalizing the reasonable truth that there are helpers who will come to anyone in earth life. This means if a person thinks it is possible, then enters the request for help, advanced spirits enter immediately to help one get the great truth of God.

Why work alone? Entirely foolish! The tender presences here who will help anyone who wants this help know how to work through the great problems of earth life, and they will lead anyone into the positive truth by helping to build a channel straight from your mind to God-mind. I have seen this work from this side, but you there will just have to accept the word of one who entered here under the assumption that God does not exist! Entering this way, I had to come to the point where I gave up my foolishness and opened myself to those who now help me."

I asked Penny if her life there is progressing.

New hope enters me now, but there is a great burden that I must work through. When we enter this plane in the way I did, we bring all our problems with us; therefore, I must team up with God-mind to work each problem through. That is what I am doing now.

Finding instantaneous tenderness that leads me into heaven is not the case. The way is tedious because I must learn and then practice bit by bit. This is my entering truth, my hope, my whole thrust for true eternal greatness.

The whole truth is here, of course, but I must one day return to earth life to try again to put my truth into the lifetime experience. The energy that I work with here is wonderful, and I want to know how to tap into it when I next go to earth life. Now I work with truth.

Teammates

26

The why's of suicide are overwhelming, especially to loved ones, friends and close associates. I asked Love about a married couple in their twenties who, according to a newspaper account, apparently believed their problems were overwhelming. Their lives ended in a murder/suicide pact.

"Outer needs permeated their whole beings," Love began. "They were teamed up with the earth truth which has its roots in physical goals. Caught up with the promotion of their prosperity, they believed their only hope was to enter their young lives into the next plane. Team up with the ones who enter here, this pair you mention. They have their own story."

The message that follows came as from one person, though perhaps it is told by both of them.

Team up with us here on this plane of life where we now reside. The pathway to a better life was possible, but we saturated ourselves with the idea that we had no hope for the future. This hopelessness was not true. We can see this by simply getting the larger view. But in the earth plane we had no larger view.

We never did believe in the God of the Universe. Our thoughts centered on our business partnership, our marriage partnership, the partnership with our family groups. But these partnerships were not reason enough to go on with life. We had the idea that we must get out of the mess we were in, the mess of the penetrating thoughts of how to succeed in business.

Also we had the persistent thought that the end of our earth lives would be like the beginning, that we would never do more than we were doing at that time. We asked ourselves, "What are we doing for others?" We did nothing. We would not even be able to have the family we wanted, for there would never be time for thoughts that would include a child. Poor business decisions were blamed on us, on our faulty judgment, our imperfect teamwork.

Now we want to get to a far place, away from the earth families who now grieve so hard. But we must stay here (close to earth) because we teamed up with what was of earth, and we must examine the whole truth of our lives there. But it isn't pleasant entering to a new plane of life, yet being subjected to the thoughts of those who were friends and loved ones. This (contact) hurts us here, but we must stay and get the whole truth that can be learned from the review of our lives and from the thoughts of others that waft to our minds here. But it isn't pleasant. The way is hard when the path is unclear.

The ones who enter to help us say we must remain here to see for ourselves what we did with our lives. They reside nearby to watch over us, to eternalize, or project, the good in our earth lives. But they insist we stay here for now. This work, and it is work, will help us team up with our new lives that we hope are ahead of us.

"Are you sorry you killed yourselves?"

No. The thoughts we had then were terrible, and they overwhelmed us. We must get new starts, right?

An eloquent pause came after this question. Were they waiting for me to respond? I waited, and then the epilogue continued.

The point seems to be that whenever one takes his or her own life, the eternal truth must be wrung from the life experience until there is nothing more to wring out. Then, and only then, we may move from this entryway between the earth plane and this plane.

I inquired if anyone there has condemned them for taking their lives.

There is no condemnation here. We meet helpers, and they lead us step by step. We know they come to help, for they eternalize what is good with our earth lives, not what is bad. We know they want to help us with this adjustment. But we had no idea that there is this teamwork available, or we would have made use of it when we were in life forms. The helpers said we could have called on them even then, and they would have helped us through the problems, whatever they were.

The helpers here say you want to use our story to put in a book where others may learn from us. The thing that we understand now that we want to tell others is that suicide need not happen to others. Our earth thoughts appeared to be bleak problems that have no solutions, but we know already that this was not true. There were ways through. Therefore, if you want to contact us from time to time, we will tell you what goes on here so we can help others.

A little over three months later, I asked again for the Teammates. "Those who come now," Love began, "come with new viewpoints. Therefore, enter their names, not as Teammates, but as Tom and Emily."

Tom and Emily

We thought our problems were the complete truth of our lives. This point of view was not entirely true, of course. But we had no perspective. We only paid attention to what was under our noses, not what was eternal truth.

The one speaking to you is Tom. I am the one who committed the murder and the suicide. I must give the whole truth not only to you but to everyone with whom I had a life relationship as well as to the God of my Being. This violent act makes me the poor truth in expression, to say the least.

The pace of Tom's report was slow and hesitant. I tried to "reach out" to him with my mind. Tom continued.

No entity has a right to take a lifetime experience away from another spirit. I am expressing my own judgment of my act. The judgment is not from others here; it is only from me. Not even Emily gives this judgment.

Everything I do now is directed toward understanding the eternal lessons that I must learn from reviewing my entire life. Even though I was a young man, I still must examine it all minutely. That way, the guides tell me, there will be no chance of repeating the petty thoughts that opened me to the murder/suicide.

Working with Tom in this way I, too, began to feel his burdens. My hands felt heavy. My fingers moved slowly. Tap—tap—tap. Words formed on the screen. I breathed deeply, reaching inside myself for new energy. Nevertheless, a lethargic feeling depressed me. Even though his energy level was waning, Tom continued.

Now that I realize the enormity of my acts, now that I know how valuable a lifetime experience is to each and every entity, the whole thing opens itself to me with the terrible clarity of one exposed to light. Therefore, now I must deal with what my guide calls "my entry into the futility of earth thought magnified."

No energy teams up with me now. The entity that I am teams up with my truth that there is the greatness of God, but now I cannot find energy. Now I need rest.

By the end of this transmission, the taps on the keys were moments apart, and when the words ceased, I felt my own energy rising. Then came a more vigorous transmission as Emily took over the message.

The one you are to call Emily is now here. The one you call Tom is resting. This rest is good for his spirit, the guide says, and there is no cause to be alarmed over his energy level. It will return when he is ready to face whatever it is he must face within himself.

I am coming into new wisdom, but I am attached to Tom's entity because we must remain together until we both unravel our mutual thoughts that brought us here in a self-imposed way. Tom was no more at fault than I, for I left it to him to kill us both because I had no eternal truth to prevent it. Therefore, I, too, must get new energy to face this same act.

What we learn now is that no problem is left behind. No problem is entered into nothingness by leaving the earth plane. In this plane the problem that we had on the earth plane simply becomes the hard rock that we must penetrate by thought. The entity who I AM now knows the rock must be dissipated, but she knows no way to do this. Tom has even given up. The guides, however, urge us forward. They remain patient, but they bring new ideas to us with persistent energy. Therefore, I have hope within me even though Tom is now asleep.

The new open truth we receive here teams up with our spirit selves easily, but the problem we have is putting that truth to work in attending to our problems. Here it is easy to receive the Pure Truth of God; it pours on us day and night -- though there is no night, actually. The Pure Truth is most welcome here because we easily see that it is the law of the land. But the only way we can ever demonstrate this truth is to enter earth life again.

It is necessary to demonstrate truth in the face of opposition. If Tom and I had given the Pure Truth sway in our lives, we would have met our problems with equanimity, with power, with an abundance of solutions. But we opened only to earth truth which preaches a doctrine of hopelessness.

The way we might now work this out is to become the truth in expression here. When the lessons are entered into our minds, we can return to earth life to be the ones who open to Pure Truth.

By contrast to Tom's message, Emily's entered rapidly, and she seemed entirely open to her situation.

The gentleness with which our guides work with us convinces us that gentleness is the way to work with one another. Gentleness is what draws me forward. No guide may force an entity to act; only by gentleness can they draw the energy of any entity into openness where they can work easily with us.

In response to my unspoken question, Emily replied.

No, there is nothing more now. If Tom were awake, he would probably want others to know that the matter of suicide is not the way to dissipate problems. Only by opening oneself to absolute truth—the kind that comes from God to each individual—can one hope to team up with the Power of Good.

The Hiram Series

27

This book contains epilogues from a teenager and a young married couple, all of whom committed suicide. Now comes an epilogue from a middle-aged man, one who was influencial in his community, one who others thought of as stable. His violent death by his own hand unsettled and haunted people's darkest thoughts and preyed upon their fears about life.

About a month after this suicide, I sought an explanation for the act from my helpful spirit friend. "How could this person, of all people, come into such despair that he would kill himself?" I asked. "Why did he do this thing?"

His wife, his children were stunned and hurt. They tried to make some sense of this act. Friends and associates wondered if some word, some friendly listening ear might have prevented this tragedy. Young adults who had admired this person felt betrayed.

The one who helps me to make contact said, simply, "This entity you open your mind to will team up with you to tell you why."

I gasped. How could I conduct an objective interview? I was among those who not only condemned the act, I even condemned the person for what I perceived as a weak and cowardly act.How could I "face" this spirit when I was being so judgmental? He would read my thoughts, know how uncaring I was, how unloving!

Nevertheless, my helper made the introduction and stated the value of our communication. "The entity whom you wish to speak to is ready with his entry now. Put the truth of what he says into clear form, for his explanations will undoubtedly help others who want to end their lives or those who have tried to do so. What he brings here will also help earthly advisers who want to help people find reasons to live."

In the following six months, I received ten separate communications from Hiram, the name he wanted me to use. His first message reflects his personality as it was in the earth plane, and he vigorously defends his suicide.

111

JUNE 27 . . .

Hiram, as this spirit later told me to call him, began.

Needs that you know nothing about provoked me to enter myself into this new place. The body teamed up with all that had no thought of good because it was not ruled by my mind (spirit). It was ruled by earth-mind truth."

How can you understand all this so quickly?

Because I have an unobstructed view. The entity who comes to help me, the one who understands all that I need to understand is my guide. This one presents the true vision that enables me to get on with my life. My mind is open now, but while I was in the body, my mind was closed.

Why would your mind open now?

To give me a clear view. Eternal truth tends to overwhelm one here. It pours out faster and deeper than I can fully understand. Either I entertain it in my mind, or else I again enter into a closed mind technique which didn't work on the earth plane.

My guide came to me immediately after I entered here to reassure me and to help me to overcome my first great fear of wrongdoing. Then I saw what I could not see while in the body form. I saw that I am a true partner with the God of the Universe. God teams up with me to become the partner of my own spirit and to help me understand what has happened.

Suicide is not recommended because it ends any chance of becoming the truth of God in practice. But in my case, this truth was shut off, and I wanted release from my body. My true being, or spirit self, wanted to end the relationship which held me to wrong thoughts. There was no thought for others in my act because I no longer held any thought of tenderness for others.

I must admit I held a hostile view toward what he told me. I felt that he was trying to justify his suicide. If he read my thoughts, he ignored them. In his earth lifetime, he was a man of great education, a person who instructed others. Perhaps he was able, because of this background, to put my thoughts aside while he continued his explanation.

I give this truth to you because they tell me here that you want to know this. They say that you work with them on this plane. This work is their teamwork, and they enter to help you become the Truth-Giver. This is undoubtedly the way it is, for no one lies here. But if you had ever told me these things while I lived in that body on earth, I would have thought you were a teacher of false teachings. Also, I would have thought you unbalanced. That was my mind set there.

It would not do any good to tell those who tenderly regarded me as the husband or the father or the friend that I live and work with you. Those who regarded me thus enter into grief, and that is the way they will work through the earthly problems of how to dispose of me. But if they could only remember the good things, they would shortcut this grief process by eternal time.

Now say what I tell you. The entity who was Hiram eternalizes that which was good in his earth life. The good remains. But the ending was not what I want remembered. Teaming up with the good, that is the whole matter now. The whole business of what was good is that which is to be remembered. That which was not too beautiful must be put away.

Still, something within me wanted to see him punished, I'm sorry to say. But the words I typed on my word processor screen were, "Have you received any condemnation for committing suicide?"

No. There is no condemnation here. The one who came to help me pictured all that I had done which was good. That way these things can be made permanent within my being, and there is growth. The rest of it falls away here.

My half angry thoughts went immediately to his wife who faced so many problems. Hiram quickly responded to my thoughts.

No. The one who was my wife would not receive you. The way she sees this second body is that the way is not clear to here, and the spirit is not understood. She must work through my suicide in her own way.

I remembered her stricken face, the hurt in her eyes, her vulnerability. Oblivious of my critical attitude, he continued.

This is my new truth—that I live in fact, not in myth or in the hope of a mysterious God.

I entered the place of pure tenderness where I know true love, true understanding, true presences who team up to help me. Here I find new truth. My old truth is already entered into the past. Therefore, now I am free to learn the reality of the universe.

Still pursuing my own thoughts about his guilt, I asked, "Aren't you sad about killing yourself and leaving all those problems behind?"

The sadness you speak of teams up with the wrong truth, you see. Sadness is not based on truth, and it is not what you want to give energy to. The person who teams up with the sadness part is not listening to what I say. The body is now dead, thank God! The body enters into dust. Death opened the door for me to enter this new, this most real and eternal life here. Get this thought straight.

There is no regret for what I did. There is only tenderness for those who grieve so bitterly. They enter into this grief to make way for new understanding. They must not enter into this strong thought of my death. They must remember only the good.

Tenderness will stay with me here, but entities there who cannot hurdle my death must work through it all on their own. That is the worst of the matter. They will enter into grief, yes. But grief is not forever.

I thanked Hiram for his communication, but he wasn't finished.

Team up with me to write the truth that I am alive here. This is most important, I think. The aliveness is important. Then write that there is no wish in my heart to undo this thing. There is no regret. The body that I occupied was weighed down with the wrong kind of truth, and to be free of that I had to enter into this plane. This is where I belong. Therefore, those who remain must do whatever they can to enter into this new relationship which lets me go to my good. They must think "good," not "bad." This part is most important. Then they will rise to great heights of spiritual growth over this thing that I have entered into.

This is all now, but there may be more if you wish to communicate with me. It might be useful to follow the process of how a spirit entity, the reality, teams up with this new life. Never think that I entered here to team up with the evil within me. I entered to team up with good. That is important to know. The body, which is refuse, eternalizes what is mostly earth-mind truth. This is clear to me from this perspective. There may be more on this as I progress. Therefore, let me help you to gather the material by entering into communication to eternalize what is not known.

In subsequent communications, Hiram came to grips with the many problems that he did not solve in earth life, problems that transferred themselves to the next plane of life. At times his emotions mingled with mine. His success was my success; his depression was my own.

JUNE 30 . . .

Three days later I told my adviser, the advanced spirit who works with this communication, that I had a feeling that Hiram was ready to speak again.

114

"There! This entity enters the place where you join up with those who wish to team up."

Hiram began without greetings or introduction to what he intended to say.

Tender thoughts go out to those whom I left there in the earth plane. They remember that which was worthwhile in my life, and they recognize my discouragement there.

They counted on one who believed there was no universal truth. I had not even considered a partnership with the God of the Universe. I stayed in tune with truth as mankind gives it. I adhered to this truth to the point where I knew there would be no point in going on with life. There was no openness on my part, and therefore, no "out" to the situation.

I did understand (while in the earth plane) that there was nothing within me except what I put in. I held some worthwhile truth, of course, but the sources I used did not offer me what I needed most. The truth I needed would have sent me to the Source of the substance of which everything is made. Why didn't I know this? Why eternalize what mankind has already proved to be not good enough?

Never team up with what is not the best in truth. The best is that which teams up with your own individual soul. The best truth is that which is absolute, that which is relevant to your own soul. I entered life to prove just that. But the entity that I was, Hiram, did not let go of old teachings (earth half truths) when the time came.

The earth truth says that a partnership with the Pure Truth is the same as the great knowledge that mankind teaches. Not so, but that is what I accepted. Therefore, every good and Pure Truth that came my way from God-mind entered a mind that rejected it. My old truth threw any possible new truth into the waste can. Therefore, the door of my being banged shut to eternalize only what I had opened my mind to.

Now I must go back over my lifetime step by step to eternalize the good. By this I mean that I must wrest the bad out of the experience until I hold only the good within me. In that way I can grow in spite of the recent way I left that lifetime. This spirit that I AM must progress, not team up with the ones with closed minds.

Yes, there are closed minds here. They reach out to invite me to join them, but I recognize them to be the very ones I wanted to help when in the earth life. That is how I know to avoid them here. When you enter here, you can join others

115

like yourself and form a partnership with those who think like you think.

Now you understand why I must study, why I must get myself into the light. Power is available here, and the truth that pours out incessantly must become my partner.

Now I work at this truth, for I want to express it. When I am more certain of myself, I will return to earth life to enter my truth into human form and then do a better job. That is my present plan. Now this communication ends to make way for the other work you do. This communication may enter again if the Brothers think this will be good. This epilogue may help others some day to open themselves to truth while in the earth life.

JULY 3 . . .

A few days later I asked again to speak to Hiram, and he was eager to resume our communication.

This is the one who was Hiram. Team up with me now to go on with our open communication about the soul's eternal quest for oneness with God.

Puzzled, I asked when we had been speaking of "oneness with God." He didn't answer my question, but went right on with his message.

Oneness with God is what I perceive life to be about here. Tenderness that I wanted in earth eternalized within me as that which gentle people in my world must give me. I did not understand what would give me satisfaction, for the tenderness I wanted looked to the earth for answers, not to the God of the Universe. Gentle presences surround me here to teach me that the love God enters into my spirit will fix the tenderness within me forever. Without this absolute true tenderness, earth life is void of this quality.

I asked Hiram if he would call his present circumstances happy.

Tenderness is what I work on now. This place is my schoolhouse. The eternalizing that I had done in earth life brought me here to this schoolhouse where I learn how to enter into the fullness of the spirit. This will come, I am assured by those who minister to me here, but I must work my way through the eternalizing until I change the earth truth into God truth, and I enter into the eternalizing of God-mind.

"How do you define 'eternalizing?'"

That which enters my mind as the way things are in reality. The eternalizing may be the truth or it may not, depending on which mind one pays attention to—earth-mind or God-mind.

I asked him if he had met anyone there whom he knew in this past lifetime.

There have been no reunions here. To have reunions, I must get tenderness within me. It has eluded me, but now I will work hard to change this theme to the expression of the tenderness of God-mind. Then perhaps I will go to the next lesson. This schoolhouse is what I need for now, not reunions. The one who helps me here (the guide) has no wish to lead me out into the tremendous world here until I graduate.

But the only way I can graduate is to grow into the spirit who may return to earth life one day to give my collected energy another try. That is all I know right now. Not much, is it? Eternal time is on my side, however. The effort I must make is before me, and the progress I have made to date is recorded. The truth of God-mind pours over me here, not only the best truth that teams up with me, but that which is needed by this person whom you call Hiram.

I asked him if he was present at his memorial service which was attended by so many people he had known, but he said he was not there.

The truth is what I must work on, not the notion of what others there open their minds to. The one who helps me here would not enter me into the earth bound stream anyway. The reason, this one says, is that I must be single minded here or else I could fall back into the earth truths.

I could open myself only to others like myself, and then I would imprison my own spirit. This will not happen if I use the advice my guide gives me. What I am doing here is getting advice and taking it as I work in this new dimension that I now am in.

I commented that what he tells here sounds as if the guide or helper is very loving.

This is true. This one who advises me brings me truth that I need so I may team up with it. This truth is not the old way, the way that leads me to despair, but the new truth that opens the door to wisdom and perfection of the spirit. This is my goal now.

"After some time, I will contact you again," I told Hiram. I explained that I wanted to wait until his spirit moves forward.

Tenderness absorbs me now. The next lesson will enter when I learn this one. But this one lesson—tenderness—is

117

the main one that my own soul needs to team up with. This may be enlightening for those in the earth plane who take no note of what the next life may be. This next life must be what we team up with in earth life.

The teacher in Hiram gave further explanation.

The theory, as I see it now, is that which I brought with me is what I am. This one who aids me says that I brought an openness that helps me now. The scientific, inquiring mind that I had to study and to learn is now what I apply to this situation. The point that I eternalize—make permanent—within my thinking self is the truth that must team up with me if I am to be a better person, a better spirit. This is my goal here.

JULY 7 . . .

Four days later, unable to get Hiram off my mind, I decided to contact him again. Perhaps he was nearby requesting another interview. At any rate, his energy was strong and vibrant as he began.

Team up with the name I now give you. The name that I enter into here is Tone of Truth.

Surely my reception was wrong!

This name is what I must be known as if I am to get the full tone of truth within my being. The thoughts of the earth entity who I was will not help me here. That lifetime is past and better forgotten here. This matter of who I AM is not relevant. The "who I AM" is the essence of "what I AM." Therefore, the "what I AM" is the Tone of Truth.

"The last time we talked you were working on tenderness as a truth within you."

Tenderness has entered me, and I know it has because I now enter into relationships here with those whom I must team up with to learn of my past lives. There is now a meeting between me and the parents I had on earth. There is much between us that needs a tender touch. This must occur if we are to let go of our earthly ties.

The tenderness lesson that I learn here will prepare me to return to earth life, but it is not the everlasting truth within me as yet. The earth life is the place where I must return to work with tenderness. When I team up with it there, I have it within me forever.

Now this soul goes its way toward those it must team up with once again.

My thoughts went to his parents.

Yes, my parents, but others too. Those whom I have not understood come toward me, those whose lives touched me in one way or another. I must enter into dialog with them, apply my new tenderness, eternalize the good between us, the spirits who had the earth relationship. This is the business of parting with what was my last incarnation. This is the way I must proceed through this place where I have the guidance, the perfect truth for my soul.

I rest a lot. This rest is to give me a chance to meditate within on the truth I am trying to make my own, not the truth that was once within me, but the new truth. Never think that it is easy here when you once enter with the eternalization of the wrong truth. That old truth overtakes me even now, unfortunately. It is like a paternal team that won't let go.

However, open truth now flows toward me to team up with me. Becoming one with truth is in my best interest, but I must make room for it. This is so hard! This part remains a problem within me. How does old truth let go? This is why I must rest now, why I must give my soul time to work through what I now understand.

I promised to give him time to rest before we communicated again.

That will be better, I think, for now there is much that I don't want to talk about. The hurt is beginning to overtake me, the hurt that I carried while on earth.

JULY 11 . . .

A few days later, however, I again sensed his presence, and I asked for Hiram. Only a moment passed before he began.

Never in my earth life did I understand why I felt such a longing for tenderness within me, but now I understand. That longing was there because I had no true tenderness concept within me. My spirit self tries now to be open, to enter into communication with others. I'm sure better truth than this is possible, but I am now on a plateau.

During my rest, my mind opened to truth and eternalized what was good in my life on earth. Getting people to enter into counseling was a positive thing. I tried to be helpful to others, and that is positive. Entering into others' great emptiness was meant to be helpful, though I didn't know how to help. The perfection I practiced when teaching was especially positive. The teamwork I gave to that work was my best.

I not only have projected the good things about my life, but I also have teamed up with those people with whom I lived. Their temperaments, their thoughts on our relationship were too much to bear for awhile. But since my rest, I can go to work again.

My counselor reminds me of the work yet to be done. This counselor reminds me too of my entire lifetime experience where I finally teamed up with total despair. I must face the wetness of the truth, but not yet.

I asked what he meant by "wetness of the truth."

The wetness descends on all Pure Truth from God-mind because earth-mind truth wants its way with each person.

I now take time to go to school to learn the value of God truth within me. We team up with this truth here, but ideally we would have teamed up with it there in the earth plane.

Then he addressed himself to "The Trilogy of Truth"*—books that were written through me. They present the Brotherhood of God who will guide anyone who asks into the God-mind connection which brings individual truth and counseling.

Get the truth books out into the marketplace, and do what you can to get them moving. These books give people the knowledge they need to understand why they team up with life in the first place.

Tenderness overwhelms me toward those I left behind to the point where I nearly enter into the lifetime experience again to try to help them. But I know so little that would help. This is my problem. The truth must take me to itself. Then perhaps I may have the wisdom to re-enter life again to help.

The two women who entered into my experience with their own tenderness have expressed their grief over me. *(He was married twice.)* To meet their own needs, they have developed their own explanations of my death. But they have no helpful idea for others who must still wrestle with grief.

The emptiness that my son feels over my death is hard to enter into, but enter into it I must until everything that he feels is my gentle truth. What tenderness opens itself to me! This tenderness is not even close to what I imagined! It helps me in one way, but it hurts me in another. But because I entered into this plane by my own hand, this kind of work is mine because the eternalization of good must also explore the depths of those whom I teamed up with. This entire process, this examination of those who were my family, will not be necessary for everyone, I am told, but it is needed by

---

**The Trilogy of Truth,* by Jean K. Foster: *The God-Mind Connection,* 1987. *The Truth that Goes Unclaimed,* 1987. *Eternal Gold,* 1988. Kansas City, Uni*Sun.

those who enter this plane as I did—if they want to make progress.

My teaching assignment in the earth life now falls to others. I see the tenderness of my fellow teachers who dilute the awful truth of my suicide. They think they do me favors by telling my students that I must have been ill, but they only avoid the truth. The students do not know whether to be afraid for their own lives—how they will meet life's problems, for example, or what. My associates should tell my students that I obviously did what was wrong. I took my own life instead of getting help in turning to the truth. But they, of course, know nothing of this truth themselves.

The great message I would give them, if I could, would be to tell them that the truth is that they enter life to be in the body, and that the great news is that their reality is spirit. Right now this is my wonderful message, but perhaps when I learn more in this temple where I study, I will have an even greater message.

I thanked Hiram for his sharing, and I said that if I could, I would share this communication with them. I added, "But they probably would not believe me—or you."

News that I live would be distracting, perhaps. But they might enter into the thought that the person who took his entity to another plane is still watching, still grinning at them, opening himself to their problems, their frustrations. This entity has not yet given up on those he served there.

News that I live might encourage some. The gentle persons who team up with the spirit concept would respond. They might feel good that I have made a transition but not an oblivion.

New gifts from the partnership with this counselor come to me now. These gifts are opening to others, entering into conversation and the interests of other entities here. Teaming up with all that enters me will not be eternalized until I get the entire concept of the God of the Universe. There is no more now.

I heed your call, and I will enter into further conversation. This eternal truth that I work with here will be one with me when I get the understanding to make it so. Teaming up with you is the way to make a record of this transition that I make.

I thought of another question which I quickly asked. "How could you identify yourself to your colleagues, your friends and your family?"

There is no need to do this, and they would not want it. The message may be helpful to someone else, but not to them. If I would try to identify myself, what would I say? I could say to each, "This is Hiram. This is the one who seemed to be one thing but was actually another. Or, this is Hiram, the one who gave you tenderness but took it away again."

Here the words came hesitantly, and we often went back to try again.

"This is Hiram who entered into great openness with you, but who returned later to learn that the only thought he had was one of depression. The openness I had with each one dissolved into great hurt by me to you." That is what I have to send to them, but I do not want to say this. Pride enters into this even yet.

I regretted the question, for answering it obviously brought pain.

But the entire work I do here depends on openness, so it is good that I tell you this. Anyway, what do I tell them to identify myself? I might say, "This is Hiram who took you to Wendy's or to other places." I could say private things, of course, the details of saying things or going here or there or some other little memory or other. But what does that matter?

The person that I was, Hiram Thorndale, (fictitious name) enters into new life, but not without the work of going over my entire lifetime experience. This is bad enough, believe me, but it is the way I must proceed. The identification is immaterial, I think. The people who would believe, believe. The others would doubt no matter what I might say. That is what I think.

AUGUST 12 . . .

It was a month before I contacted Hiram again. My thoughts went out to him many times, and I hoped all went well with him. With much enthusiasm, I looked forward to our next contact.

"May I speak to the entity who was Hiram?" I asked, and without introduction or greeting, he began his message.

The work that I do now enters every open crack of my lifetime experience.

The words tumbled through my mind and out onto the word processor screen.

The work that teams up with me is to examine each of those cracks with microscopic thoroughness. The eternalizations that I made while living in the earth plane play their part in this examination, for I must examine them to learn why I made them. This is what the teamwork insists on my doing now.

"By teamwork," I asked, "do you mean you and your guide?"

Yes. The guide and I form a team who work to help me grow into the open spirit who can absorb God truth.

My thoughts frequently pass this judgment upon my life: The entity who I was never opened himself up to others. He entered into no open expression with anyone, not even those he told his thoughts to. Others entered his lifetime experience, but the one who was Hiram entered into no exchange of valuable thought.

Remember, we get Hiram's understanding as he gets it, little by little. We must follow his experience through his eyes, through his perceptions.

The lesson I must learn is that those who live in the earth plane must participate in an exchange of thought. I interpret this lesson as the gift of the God spirit—that we clothe ourselves in the truth about the exchange of good thoughts so that in the next lifetime we will not make the same mistake. But I am sure there is more to learn about this matter. I touch the surface, as it were. The cracks go deep into the experience, and I am only at the top part.

The truth that I get here exists to help me, but it can penetrate only as far as I allow it. Of course I do the best I can, but it is very hard, and I inch along in the process much as the caterpillar who sets out to encircle the world. This gives you an idea of how slowly I go.

I asked Hiram if he still had a guide.

Yes. My guide patiently enters into my being where we communicate at a level I never knew was possible. This communication enters my being with an energetic thrust that teams up with God Himself. Yet I have not opened those cracks very wide! This sounds impossible, doesn't it? Yet entering those cracks that I filled with eternal concrete is not easy. They need the blast of my open mind, but this openness is still underway.

The telephone rang, and reluctantly I thought, "excuse me," and went to answer it. After the call, I had to leave the house for about thirty to forty minutes. My mind fretted over the delay, for I wanted to get back to the rest of the communication.

"I'm here, finally!" I signaled to Hiram.

Never think that we on this plane have the time element you do. The time you team up with is not ours. Therefore, when you said "excuse me" and left, it was but a moment to me. A warp of some kind enters into this plane, a holding pattern that keeps everything in an entirely different thought time. If this doesn't make sense to you, it is because it isn't clear to me yet. When I understand it, perhaps I can explain it better.

"I have heard," I began, "that it is easy to create things there— houses, gardens, anything. Are you doing any creating?"

"No. My thoughts now are directed to my past life. The present time is not even open to me. But when I get the lessons learned, the examination completed, I will then team up with whatever awaits me here.

This plane is not reflecting the earth truth I once employed. That's why I must edge into it slowly, cautiously, teaming up only when I get the next lesson completed. The plane I am in is open to my perusal, but I cannot join in with its activity yet.

There are those, as I said before, who want me to join them, but I recognize them as people who also had problems in the earth plane. They reject a guide and want to cling together to have whatever it is that such clinging brings them. But not for me! Entering here as I did, I want to open myself to a better life, not the same or worse.

SEPTEMBER 13 . . .

Another month went by before I again asked to speak to Hiram. This time there was an introduction, as if I were meeting a spirit I had never known.

"A tender expression of goodwill teams up with you when this entity enters to speak to you. Eternalizing his own truth, he now presents a new teammate who enters with his new truth." Hiram *began immediately.*

No one who enters this eternalization of truth will turn away empty-handed. When I was in earth life I never thought that God truth could be the open-ended, tremendously good truth that it is. The oneness I now feel with this truth is my touchstone which eternalizes good thoughts. The wholeness I now feel is the result of the truth that is my own. The tenderness I needed to express is now eternalized within me, with the exception of what crystallizes within me on the living of my past life. No one entering my presence here would recognize the one who called himself Hiram.

The purpose of my communication with you enters a new phase now. The first phase was to tell you what happened after the eternalization of hopelessness and despair. Then I told of the truth that helped me to evaluate my past life and to learn its lessons.

All this was a very hard experience, but now I awake, so to speak, to new horizons. The open-ended truth that I am in the process of becoming will soon be permanent within me. What I mean by open-ended truth is truth that is open to what I may become. There is no end to possibilities. This is why I enter today so happy and sending good thoughts to you.

The entity that I was sent thoughts to you that he felt along the way. When the first phase ended successfully, I was entered into the next phase. That is the way it goes. The true guide who helps me here was right on every count. I expected this progress at the beginning, and I determined to do exactly as this advanced spirit suggested.

In answer to my fleeting unspoken question, Hiram replied.

No. This spirit never ordered me to do anything. I knew I had a choice which had to be honored. It was in my mind that this was so. Perhaps I knew from previous experience. I'm not sure. But I knew that I must pay strict attention to this guide or I would be lost. That is why I followed every suggestion this entity gave me, and that is why I have progressed so fast.

I now am ready to present further truths to you to put into the book, truths which may help others who despair over their lives.

The teacher self of Hiram emerged here to catalog his new understanding and the next phase of our work together.

Now! The first thing we shall take up is the purpose of this entity that I AM, this spirit self. My purpose is to become one with the God of the Universe. This oneness is the perfect expression of greatness, the perfect expression of all that every spirit would want to be or to demonstrate. That is why expressing as one with God is so exciting to me. This truth is mine!

The second thing I want to express is my certainty of the eternal goodness that prevails when we open our hearts to it. Goodness prevails here, and I can see it prevails in the earth plane, too, when people turn their minds to this concept. Eternal goodness, one aspect of God, will team up with those who turn their minds to this concept. Open your mind, open your heart, open your entire being to goodness, and that is what you will experience in both planes. Give this thought your best energy, for there is nothing more important, is there, than eternal goodness? When we turn to this understanding, the partnership with it is complete, and we therefore demonstrate it in our lives.

The third thing I want to present today is my own version of what death is. The entity that I was took the opportunity to enter into death deliberately, but this entity that I was

125

thought he would end all problems. Death was welcomed. But the truth was not known to him.

The truth is that this entity entered the next plane of life much the same as he departed the earth plane! What a disappointment! There I, the entity that I was, teamed up with the desperate problems that I had before I eternalized death. The wetness (of the truth) that I had experienced in the earth plane still plagued me in this plane. Hopelessness pursued me, poor vibrations gave me eternalizations of poverty of spirit. Nothing had changed! This thing called "death" had not brought me the expected peace of mind.

Nothing had changed. Think of that! Nothing had changed. "Betrayed by my own hand," I thought. Tormented by my own inability to function in earth life, the entity who entered this plane tried to enter into thoughts of temporary peace, but nothing worked. Then came my benefactor, my guide who came to give me hope.

This guide opened my mind to his by way of thought, and the thought inspired me to become open to this advanced spirit. Goals were presented to me, goals that I could accept and meet to become what I probably wanted to become, one with God.

The other side of the picture was also presented, but neither side teamed up with me at first. The second picture the guide gave me was that I could team up with those who, like me, found the lifetime experience too much to bear, and therefore, entered into this plane by their own hand. This group of entities, the guide told me, would welcome me to become one with them, and they would invite me into their fellowship.

Never did I think I wanted to join with others like myself. The blind leading the blind, the poor teaching the poor, the getters of pain trying to help other getters of pain. That would be the destiny of my soul if involved with others like me. Therefore, I emptied my hopelessness then and there, telling the guide that if I could be given an outlook to a better life, I would go that way.

That is what happened, and I entered into this close association with the guide who helped me to enter into the pure thought of God Who enters my being to teach me the truth for my soul.

Now the work has progressed a long way. The time has now come for me to enter into the higher reaches of truth, but there is one obstacle. The truth must be proved, and no one proves truth here. The truth must be proved in the lifetime expression there in the earth plane. That is the way people grow—in the earth plane. As for me, and others who enter here as I did, we grow by putting truth within our beings to the point where we can return to earth life again.

Getting to this point is my present assignment. Therefore, I go forth, still with my guide, to help others. When I mature sufficiently, the guide will enter into work with someone else and leave me to the work that I can then do on my own.

Transfixed, I absorbed the words that poured through, and Hiram took note of my concentration.

Yes, this is fascinating. Who would have ever believed all this? The earth plane boxes people in to the point that they are not open to this next plane of life at all.

I interrupted Hiram's outpouring to ask if any punishment is meted out to people who commit suicide?

No one speaks of punishment. This thought exists in the earth plane, I guess, but not here. The truth is the stated element here, the truth that we must become one with and which we must express in the lifetime experience. If we do not do it one time, we go again to try. This is the way it is as far as I can tell.

Again I stopped the transmission. "When we last communicated," I said, *"you were entering into the thoughts of those you loved in this earth plane, and you were despondent about what you found. How did you resolve all this?"*

Thoughts that gave me pain showed me that the people I had thought did not care really entered into the purest kind of caring for me. That was the truth that was hardest to bear, the truth that altered my own progress. Why would anyone want to repeat such a thing? Would I ever want to repeat this misadventure? No! The next lifetime experience must be one of demonstrating tenderness to the point of being noted as the tender person whom everyone notices as that quality.

"Were you surprised about reincarnation?"

Reincarnation gives me hope to overcome my problems. And it gives me hope that those who hurt because of me will also overcome their pain and have more lifetimes that will be happy. Reincarnation is the better outlook, the more hopeful and optimistic outlook.

Yes, I was surprised, but when I get to the point of putting my recent lifetime in perspective, I am told I will remember my other lives, and that it will be more natural to express myself as the sum total of all my lifetimes. Now I am still tied in to the last lifetime experience.

EPILOGUE

"You sound very optimistic," I told him. "I wish those you knew in the earth plane could read this."

No, it would not connect with them at all. They hold no such ideas, and I know because I was one with them just a short time ago. The tenderness I team up with now enters into a partnership with all that I am now, not the way I was then. These who were my compatriots would only object to your saying these words came from me, and they would ridicule it all. They would need to do this or else they would be proved wrong in their own evaluations of themselves and of me. They have long since entered their own observations about my life and my death, and they want no more on the subject. That way they will not have to reevaluate themselves. But I do not worry over this at all.

When I grow more advanced, perhaps I can help to turn them toward truth. The guide said this is sometimes possible when people who team up with the truth want to help earth entities. When this is possible, I will work. Meanwhile, I work here on myself only. That is the whole thrust now, to move toward the goal of oneness with God.

There was a pause, and then a final word.

The truth expands me to the point where you find me today, relatively happy, right? The energy that I generate is that which emanates through the Pure Truth of God which flows into and through my being. What blessed relief from despondency, from despair, from hopelessness that I entertained both in earth life and when I came here.

OCTOBER 14 . . .

After last months's vigorous and inspired communication, I looked forward to the next message. However, Hiram's enthusiam was replaced by a thoughtful, slower, more studied approach.

Team up with me today in the beauty of this worthwhile endeavor we enter into. The problems that I brought here, the overcoming problems that caused me to take my own life, entered here with me. Therefore, the hope of getting rid of them is not possible at all. The truth of this statement is what I must explain the best I can.

The problems which one puts into permanent form in the lifetime existence on earth must be worked through there, or they enter here in this next plane to be overcome. What can I do, for example, about financial problems here? The truth enters me now about how to overcome the problem of financial necessity, but I must execute this truth in an earth life if my spirit self is to grow.

128

Take the problem I had in relationships. Now I see with unbelievable clarity what was wrong there. But what good does that do me now that I cannot overcome those problems on earth?

The entering truth is wonderful, yes, but the fact of my unwillingness to team up with this truth while in earth life makes me have the entire problem here.

There were other problems too, of course. I, who entered this plane at my own hand, wanted to have the respect of my peers. They gave me this respect, but yet they gave me their objections too. The person that I was then had no way to evaluate what they returned to me, and finally the idea came that I was generally disliked. Would you think this would still be a problem for me? Well, it is, for when I got here and returned to visit those with whom I worked, I knew their hearts. They had great respect for my work, more than enough for any one person. Yet I did not enter into this at all while I was there.

Another situation I faced was that the entire earth seemed teeming with problems. I wanted peace. I wanted an expression of tenderness among the people in the world. But all I saw was war. These problems extended to my person, to my most intimate part where I felt rejected because I wanted peace and there was no peace! Can you understand this thing I tell you?

I forgot no hopelessness while I lived in the earth plane. Entering God truth fell on deaf ears. That was the major problem, but I did not see it. Joining up with negative forces as I did, determining the worst in things, the most horrid in life, I felt no hope. The depths I explored are better left forgotten, for they had no opportunity to wane and to give way to what is optimistic and good.

Nothing else that expresses within me now can erase these objects I hold here. I say "objects," for they seem hard and heavy and will not dissipate. That is the immediate understanding I have now. The only way I see through all this is to enter into earth life again with greater truth inside me, truth that will give me the power to vaporize these wet truths from earth and replace them with the gentle truth that God gives.

Tenderness that has crept into my being here has awakened me to these points I bring up here. Before the tenderness took hold of me, I could not have seen these things.

The words stopped, and after a moment of silence, Hiram continued.

EPILOGUE

The one who guides me tells me that I am now working to dissipate these awful problems.

The thing I must do is to work with others who come here because they took their own lives. This work is no fun, but I do it because my guide says I may learn to overcome these problems to the extent that they will bring themselves under the powerful energy that is the laser beam of God. He then will use this beam to open each problem to the light which will put each problem into open truth where it may enter the optimum power that will let them fade.

Even I, who tells you these things with authority, do not understand how this works. But like everything else that has happened since I came here, I am ready to learn and open myself to new truth. The "old truth" would be more like it, I expect.

The one that I am now, the one I call Tender Truth Entering into Expression, will now tell you why I want to participate in this book. The reason is that every time I work to bring perspective into my situation here, I need more truth. The need is necessary if I am to attract the new truth. Our work in this book will help, I hope, to put the matter of suicide into the perspective of eternal truth. And this perspective, when read and accepted, will help others to work out their problems while in their earth lives.

Entering into this plane provides no reasonable answer to any problems. If the problems would disappear, then the matter would be closed, and then suicide would be a good thing. But the way these problems of mine have teamed up with the interminable thoughts of a lack of solution—well, I know that I have left the problems on one plane but recreated them here. They will stay with me until I team up with the truth of how to disperse them—every last one of them.

Helping others, as I said, helps me. And telling you, the readers of this book, the way it really is here when you enter by your own hand, helps me too, though I don't exactly understand why. My way is now lighter and brighter than it was in the beginning. But I see for a fact that it is not as easy to start over as I thought it was the last time I reported on my life here.

Therefore, though this message is somewhat shorter, and though it is somewhat more into the problems I have, the truth of my state must be told. No use in glossing over the life here. No use in giving false hope to others. The truth enters to give its own challenge.

Team up today with the truth-givers of your time, those who write about the truth of the universe, those who write what God gives them to write. Then go to those who can help you—the advanced spirits who abound on this plane to bring help to each one who asks for help. Get your own truth. Enter into it to use it and to bring it into focus there. Then you enter here without your problems entering with you.

This is my message at this point. But there may be more. Entering truth pours onto me now since I have given these words. Entering truth pours over me, and there is a helper here who will teach me how to use it.

NOVEMBER 19 . . .

When I asked for Hiram next time, I was greeted by one of the Brotherhood of God, an advanced spirit who has worked with me since I began writing the truth trilogy.

"The one who tells you his own story comes with regularity to report on the situation, and he progresses past even our best expectations. He enters his thoughts with honesty, not with hidden intent. Therefore, we want you to use as much of his story as you can to show the forward thrust of his entity. The one now called Hiram is our candidate to become the symbol of how those who enter this plane of life can work with advanced spirits to further growth toward what all want in truth—to be one with God.

"This oneness is a matter of being open, being ready to enter new truth, new eternalizations. This one, whom you now speak to concerning his ongoing experience, teams up with the best that is here, the way to perfection.

"Put this story to paper where it will encourage all who read it, where it will team up with those who wonder why everything in their lives seems to be going wrong. This one will stand in the annals of this cooperative writing as the one who opens doors for those who have closed their spirits to the truth of God-mind. Team up with his person as he works with great energy to right the wrongs he perceives he has committed by working with you in this, his best endeavor.

"He is not the entity he was on earth. He is now in the energy of the perfection that is God. Here he is."

Gentle presences team up with me here to urge me to continue to write with you about my life here in this plane. The truth here opens my mind to the wonderful possibilities I had when I entered earth life. Though there were possibilities, not many materialized into fullness. The reason, of

131

course, is that earth-mind truth got hold of me as that which was right, that which would lead me to success.

I gave my teamwork to earth-mind truth, and here is the reason. The energy that is of earth-mind whirls over the earth plane entering all who hold their attention to it. I gave it my attention because it indeed seemed wonderful, to be perfectly honest. Earth-mind truth came into being because mankind perverted the original truth of God-mind. The half truths, and the untruth all became earth-mind truth. Therefore, I gave my attention to the truth that led inevitably to my destruction.

Now you see why none of the best truth prevailed within me. The tenderness I always wanted while in earth life perverted itself to receiving tenderness from my friends and family, not from the Gentle Being which is Tenderness. Let me explain. The Gentle Being which is Tenderness is the God of the Universe. This one who offers me (or anyone) this gift is ready to hand it over upon request, and in this way tenderness is within me, within my being, my spirit self. My longing is met in this way. I would not need to reach and reach for tenderness from others when I AM tenderness.

None of my goals, hopes and dreams in earth life were open to God's great truth. They were of earth-mind. The greatness which is of God needed to be put at the core of my being. Then I would have rejected any truth that led me into final despair and ideas about destroying my body.

Now I see the entire situation clearly, but then, face to face with it, I did not see anything worthwhile. What I have learned is this: Team up with the truth within your own being, the truth that calls forth to the God of the Universe. This truth is what one brings to earth life. We all know we are of God, but many turn away from this thought. The energy of God enters earth life, and it calls for the open communication direct to God-mind.

The earth truth, however, turns people away from this thought. "What a fool," this truth says. "Imagine getting truth straight from God!"

I knew a witness who got truth straight from God, but I misunderstood him. The witness was the one named Jesus. He was never presented to me as one who became one with God. Rather, he was presented as the one who was God when he was born. Therefore, I did not identify with Jesus at all.

Now entering truth has revealed to me that Jesus was one of many who teamed up with the God of the Universe while

132

in earth life in order to bring others into the proper understanding of their own potential. This truth I have stated is
here on this plane so that all who enter here might understand. But what is needed is that same understanding on the
earth plane.

Walking on water—that is not just an eternalization of
Jesus, but it is the possibility open to all mankind. What
wonderful thoughts penetrate me now! What possibilities
enter my mind. Too late for my last lifetime, yes, but not too
late for my next lifetime.

The one that I Am, that is, the one who enters to express
his truth, is not the same one who entered this plane a while
ago. This one that I Am, the Hiram which I named myself,
is ready to become energy in expression. That means that I
am ready now to fully express God-mind because I see how
this energy focuses in the earth plane to wrest away the half
truths or the untruths.

Entering into communication with you, I eternalize what
I must in order to move into new truth. Those whom I now
help (in this plane) end up helping me. These who gave
themselves to suicide all help me to be the one I want to be.
My entering truth helps me to help others here, and, of
course, it helps me too.

Those who enter here because they opened themselves to
earth-mind truth enter without hope. They want to know
what manner of place this is, as I did. This new work of mine
is the right thing for me now. How long it will go on I do
not know. Those whom I left on the earth plane remember
me and grieve, but they would not know me now. They
would not even think I resemble the one they knew there.

Now entering this earth plane to speak with you I can even
see how it was there, even how I felt there. The earth-mind
truth tries to penetrate me yet.

*Here Hiram stopped, and the following words were spoken hes-
itantly, slower and slower to the end.*

Never will this truth let up, I suppose, but yet there is
hope to make it better. Entering God-mind truth becomes
part of this bank of earth truth whenever those in the earth
plane give themselves to the expression of God-mind truth.
That is why those advanced spirits here want you to demonstrate your truth. The way to make earth-mind rise in
vibration—which is to say, help it to become better—is to
put the God-mind truth into the everyday fabric of earth life.

Here is my guide who says that I must get to my work here. There are newcomers who need my help, so I now go with this advanced one.

DECEMBER 15 . . .

I asked to speak to the entity who was Hiram in his last earth life. Love replied, "The one who enters is ready to open to you on the subject of his worthiness as a truth eternalizer."

The one who tells you this is my guide, my helpful advisor, the one who has opened the truth of the universe to me. This one has my entire attention, my gratitude and my affection. My guide has an open channel at his command, and through him I am learning to build that open channel too. This means that I can now receive the truth of God-mind. This God truth will entitle me to move toward my goal here— getting ready to return again to earth life.

A question formed in my mind.

No, it isn't too soon, Truth-Giver. The entity that I Am wants to return to open my truth to earth. With new truth within me, I can move back into earth life to create the kind of teamwork that will enter into the goodness of God. This truth enters to prove that I AM that One with God, that One with all that is teamed up with universal good, all that is of Pure Truth. The greatest goal I have right now is to return ready to enact the truth.

No entering truth has discouraged me. I know that I must return, and I do not mind that. In fact, I welcome it. The way I will progress is by accomplishing my new plan. This is my one overpowering goal, you see. The positive thrust of this truth is to help me accomplish this.

The entire open truth pours to my truth center, my spirit which is now tuned in to receive what God-mind has to tell me. It is the not-so-secret way I have of opening my being to the truth. The way is not hard, but it took me awhile to find it, you see.

The only thing that is important is that wetting (throwing cold water on) God truth will result in the obsolete teamwork I used before to no avail. The God truth was there to perceive, yet, I could not avail myself of it. Therefore, I put forward as truth what was actually only earth-mind truth. There was some good in it, of course, but it entered without getting itself united with what is the Partner—the God of the Universe, the One Who is both the Gift and the Giver, the Principle, the Law, the Teammate who will work within each one to accomplish the potential. That is what I left out, and without this Partner, there is no essential power.

I asked if he had anything else to add.

This intended thought must be added. Our work together is not entirely honest unless the following point is made. The new worth that I now feel within me is, in part, due to this communication which helped me to give my own truth to those still in earth life. Therefore, I send you the thought of gratitude that you have entered into this communication.

The way to truth is by way of the open channel, the Christ of each one. And the truth that God-mind channels into your inner being will team up with you to make your lifetime experience one of joy that really does pass all understanding—as you now think of joy in earth terms.

The way to do this? The teamwork here on this plane includes those who turn to help you each minute of every day. They, this special group of advanced spirits, this Brotherhood of God, wait for your request. They stand ready to help you with every problem, every tender point of your life. The best thing they do, however, is to show you how to build that channel from your being to God's Being. Then you do what every wise person must do—open your mind and your heart to the Source of Everything.

With this advice, Hiram, the consummate teacher, concluded his extensive epilogue concerning his ongoing lifetime in the next plane. He is obviously not the same entity as the one who began this series. I have tried to visualize him as he is there—a new body by now, a new expression, a new way of presenting his being.

In his last lifetime he was vigorous, lithe, devoted to good health—both mentally and physically. Yet, Hiram did not find life worth living. Now, however, I can see him in my mind's eye, greeting those who arrive in the next plane after killing their bodies. They must be desolate and unhappy, some fearful of judgment, others running to hide, perhaps. No doubt Hiram strides forth to these who feel broken, and he brings them hope and tenderness.

"The newness of his spirit becomes the open ended truth in motion," his guide announced to me. "This one who was Hiram now brings his eternal wisdom to team up with those who can lead him into perfection. This entity, this spirit, this mind is the epitome of what any spirit entering here can team up with. His growth is the result of the teamwork that is of God, the individual and the advanced spirits who help each arriving spirit."

An Afterword By the Brotherhood of God

28

"To you, the reader, we give a message of hope. We will come to you even now while you are in earth life to give our assistance to those of you who want the absolute truth for your spirit. We who unite under the arm of God enter your being if you want us, and we enter to help you make the most of your lifetime experience.

"The entire thrust of this book is to present tender truth for your quiet reflection. Eternal truth teams up with you today because you have opened to the epilogues in this book, but entering truth that is just for your own spirit self must be requested. Those of us who work with this writer will team up with you whenever you want this truth. We stand ready, but we do not enter without your request.

"The teamwork that is possible for you here is that which will put you into the truth of the God of the Universe. Then you will know the wisdom of God, and you will march to no other drumbeat. Your life will prosper beyond your greatest hopes, and you will enter into this next plane of life unafraid and eternalizing the wonder and tenderness that will greet you."

ESSAYS
29

"I wonder . . ." precedes many questions concerning life, death and what happens to our spirit selves. The following essays are answers to many such queries posed by people who have read the preceding epilogues. The material comes from advanced spirits in the next plane of life, those who call themselves the Brotherhood of God.

What do we do in the next plane—just learn truth?

The question is not phrased exactly right. Everyone needs new God-mind truth, but many already have much of this truth within them. Why do they need more? Here is the real question.

The eternal truth that is instated within one's soul is indeed useful. This truth holds a person to the plan that was brought to this earth life. That anyone should spend extensive time in the next plane relearning what is already known is not at all purposeful, is it?

Therefore, it is well to understand that when one arrives here with God truth instated, we, who guide the spirits newly arrived, will redirect the one who does not need this plane's work into a more appropriate plane where he can work at whatever he wishes. The fertile and creative part goes with him, and he will open himself to many new and interesting thoughts in the plane he enters.

The next plane of life, from where we speak with you, is only the first of many, many planes. The planes are not teamed up with the idea that one is higher or better than another, but they are teamed up with the idea that wherever the spirit is in development, there is an appropriate plane of activity.

The place where you will live and work, the plane that is open to you in this better expression of life, will provide you with opportunities that you cannot even imagine now. Therefore, open yourself to the understanding that there is no way that all of you go through exactly what the entities presented in this book go through.

You are each unique; you are in different stages of development. In the entering plane you will learn where you should be, and you will, along with your guide, make decisions for your growth and advancement. The perfect way is provided here because the God of the Universe prevails in His greatness, His perfection, in His teamwork with all who want to be one with Him.

Therefore, hope for the best that existence can be, for you are sure then to receive the highest and the best. The lifetime experience in earth may be good, but the way we view things here, it is but the training ground for the advancing soul. Team up with the Brotherhood to learn how to connect to God-mind, and we will open the many doors of possibilities for you.

Can we live on other planets?

Those spirits who enter into earth life want the human experience just as you know it. But those who go to other planets want the kind of experience that particular planet affords. Though you may not understand perfectly, try to give it your esteem.

The God of the Universe works with the process of gently opening matter to the form that would best contribute to the overall good of the entire universe. To team up with His purpose, you might want to put yourself into that planet as a teammate who works with God in His process, whatever it is. This way you would learn the value of teamwork.

The ultimate expression, however, is being able to stand in the earth plane with those around you who may or may not help you in your spiritual growth, and grow in spite of it all. A lifetime experience is the way to advance to the point where you need not return to earth again. You will then be free to advance to other work, other experiences.

Why does an elaborate system of planes and planets exist?

This elaborate system of planes and planets enters into the overall creative plan that God sends into the open void. That there should be emptiness and God is not feasible. That there

140

should be nothing in the great vast space when God is working His eternal truth is not teamed up with understanding.

Where there is God, there is creativity. Where there is God, there is the ongoing way to perfection. That God could operate in a void is not only without eternal truth, it is without the purpose of the great intelligence that is at the heart of this God.

Is God real?

Real? The spirit is real, my friend. The spirit is indestructible, ongoing, tangible in the sense that it is the part of you that becomes the reality on this plane next to earth plane.

That God only sends thoughts of a vague unreality is only the way it seems in the earth-mind where this idea festers. God is not seen by earth eyes because God is in evidence to the point where His greatness overwhelms your own ability to see Him. The ant that crawls right up to your finger and then proceeds on its way up your arm has no idea that he is aboard a huge human being who can crush it in a moment. If he could see you, he would run. You are too huge for that ant to see.

Eternal truth pushes through to the earth plane to give you some concept of God, but there are many who do not even see this truth in motion right there in their midst. They cry out, "There is no God," when the truth they should cry out is, "I am blind! I am indeed blind."

God is the only reality that eternalizes in the wide universe. If you feel it necessary to see this God, you hold such a small concept of Him that it is hardly worth commending. God is too vast for you, too great for you, too much for your understanding and certainly too much for your poor eyesight! Therefore, turn within to the temple of your being and there and only there can you meet this One of whom we speak.

Why doesn't God make us perfect?

The way to perfection is not through a giant operating of power that overwhelms and subdues you. No! What kind of creatures would you be if you were subdued to no questions, no reactions, no ideas of working through understanding on your own? Would a great God, a God of perfection, want creatures that were molded by one thrust of power? Would He want entities to sit there and be played with like dolls? Would he want those who inhabit the universe to rise to great heights of nothingness? The question surely reflects poor understanding!

141

God is that overriding thrust of moving intelligence, of greatness that pours energy into creative functions. We, you the reader and we who aid in the writing, team up to become God's workers in a vast field of energy. To understand our own greatness, we must first understand how to become one with God in the forward movement of the creative process. Then we may be the ones to work as teammates with· God, to be His tenderness in expression, His wholeness in expression, His perfection in evidence.

How can we become One with God?

The only way to be one with God is to forthrightly team up with Him. That is the answer. There is no way to be one with God if you persist in riding the waves of opinion on the subject. There is no way to become one with Him if you write your vast opinion on the subject for public exploration. There is no way to become one with God when you team up with one another to talk about God and go away feeling happy that you talked. No, the only way to be one with God is to move toward the target—God!

Opinions do not matter. Your teammates in the earth plane may or may not help you in your journey, but do not rely on them. The strength of groups may eternalize tenderness among the group, but it does not put you into oneness with God. What we say to you in every way, every thought, in every word, is that God is the reality of the universe. To be one with that reality is to put yourself into the thrust of great energy, great open truth, tender growth of spirit.

Be involved with new truth that comes to you from God-mind. Team up with what is of value to you, not to others. Bring your open mind to be filled, your open heart to be understood and given its needs. Team up with this wonderful God by opening your mind, opening your heart and by turning to those here who can help you to make the giant step forward to connect with God-mind.

That is our message, our tender expression to you of what can surely change your life for the better.

Do fixed expectations help us deal with the next plane?

Those who come to this plane expecting Jesus to welcome them with open arms and promises upon his lips are always disappointed. Those who enter with any fixed expectation never rise to meet the reality of this plane without our help.

The ones who enter here expecting to open their hearts to God Himself have the wrong thoughts entirely. They enter believing that God is a man who lives in heaven. What a ridiculous notion! The God of the Universe is not held within one planet, let alone within one entity. Those who expect to see God only receive empty thoughts of disappointment, and thus they close themselves off to any help.

Those who wait to receive the thought projection of their poor truth will bypass our entire teamwork. They will not know where to turn or what to do, but inevitably they will refuse help. Why? They already know the way; they know everything! They team up with their own egos that proclaim them as experts in the spiritual realm.

There are also those who come with the firm expectation that there is no life after death. Those, too, enter here and refuse help because they team up with their earth-mind thoughts that tell them that since they had not seen or heard God in their earth lives, there is no God. Therefore, whatever is happening to them in this plane must not be real. They actually believe they are in some time lapse or some thought fixation produced by problems in dying. They turn away from the tender help of the guides and empty their thoughts on barren substance. They proclaim emptiness, nothingness, and they produce what they think with such passion.

There are some who enter this plane and refuse to review their lifetime experience and attend to all those matters that were unresolved. Until they make this review, they cannot move forward.

They firmly believe, you see, that this plane is already perfected for them. They revert to their belief system that says there has been a mistake. They expected no problems, but yet they appear to have problems. "How can this be?" they think. "How will we get away to the wonderful peace we want?"

The answer to both these questions is, of course, that each soul must work within the law or principles of God. Then each spirit self may understand what is happening and will know how to progress past the beginning point where death has deposited them.

Can we tap into creative truth?

No one who wants the Truth of Our Being will be denied it. What you want to know is how people in the creative arts can attain the truth that will enable them to work effectively in these fields. Hear, oh hear, those who want to create music, those who want to create the eternal truth about the beauty they see and the beauty they feel!

Those who want to bring music to the earth may tune in here to this plane where music abounds. They may enter into that which is basic to creativity, no matter their earth preparation. There are writers of music who know nothing of composition, nothing of theory. Then there are many who know much of composition, much of the theory that lies at the base of putting notes together, but they still do not enter into great composition. Why?

The answer lies within that person, within that individual who opens himself to the powerful thought concept of music that enters into reality in this plane. Those who enter earth because they want to open themselves to the creative arts do so with their growth plan laid out. There it is—the plan by which they will eternalize whatever it is they wish to eternalize, whatever they wish to put before the world. They knowingly enter earth plane with the basic knowledge instilled within them. Then they put their art into evidence, and others stand amazed.

Why be amazed? The plan they made here on this second step of life, this plane where the spirit enters and reviews its life, where the spirits gather who ready themselves to return to earth, is to be enacted. Why marvel that this is so?

When you put understanding into your being, you may then rewrite your own plan that you made before you came to the earth plane. What you put into it is what you most want to accomplish? Perhaps you have a secret or not so secret desire to put your energy into the creative arts. What stops you? What turns you to whatever it is you do now? Why not tune in to this plane where the ready energy teams up with your plan?

The one who originally asked this question of the writer wants to enter into understanding that has been eternalized within him. He wants to know with his earth brain what his mind has already told him. The truth that enters to be used is that which your own being calls forth. We here in this plane marvel—tenderly, of course—that so many people believe they have limited worth in their eternal beings. Why do they hold this limitation? Why do they enter into the limitation idea that holds them back from the accomplishment of their dreams?

Yes, what you read here is absolutely true. There is no desire here to hide this truth. The teamwork possible to you may bring you the best thoughts you can imagine when you deliberately tune in to the art that interests you most. Yet, when you tune in, there is no sense of you putting forth something that another opens to you. No, you merely tune in to the best of basic worth. Then, with your interest within you, perhaps your training, perhaps only your consuming passion without training, you take this basic worth and use it to produce the creative genius that opens whatever it is to the earth plane.

Teaming up with those in this plane who team up with you upon request is what you must do now if you believe that your growth plan has gone awry. Perhaps you are the one who began by writing music. Then the inspiration began to fade. Or perhaps you were the writer who believes now he or she is "all written out." Team up with those in this plane who hold their minds open to you, who send their thoughts to you to begin now to replenish your mind with that which will put you back into your plan.

Can work/career help achieve spiritual goals?

The value of work is not applicable to the growth of spirit. The earth lifetime expresses whatever truth the spirit has brought with it, but there is no precise pattern to follow regarding the selection of work or career. The choice is up to you. The main thrust of your lifetime must be to *put your own personal truth into expression.*

What you do is important insofar as it relates to your personal satisfaction. In that way, the truth impacts upon your choice of work. Then the truth will, if you let it, help you to give your time to work that relates to great personal satisfaction. In this way, you will be bringing truth to bear upon your lifetime experience, right? In this way you will grow because you have used truth in the way it is supposed to be used.

The work you choose is not given tremendous importance, nor is it regarded as more or less than what others do. What is important is to wrest your truth into expression, either through your work or through other activities. There is no judgment upon your work.

The other side to your work experience is, of course, whether or not you use God truth to bring utmost value into your work. How do you spend it in your life? Do you put greatness into your work? If not, you become only the earth-mind expression who works to be paid. Those who work only for pay never know happy satisfaction. The work place is either an expression of Pure Truth which results in all you want and expect, or it teams up with earth truth that produces no great joy or greatness.

145

EPILOGUE

Work places are a mixture of expectations, but you have the key to what happens there in regard to your satisfactions. That key is God truth. And you hold that key within you.

How can we get perfect wisdom?

If you want to know anything in the universe, and you open yourself to the energy that is available to you, you will enter into wisdom.

Team up with this understanding that you may learn the truth of whatever matter you lay before the Source of Truth. Teamwork is the key to learning all things. This teamwork begins within you, within your spirit self, within your being. Then it extends to the team of those who reside in the next plane of life to help you to direct your Pure Thought into the energy that you require.

Then, the One God Whose entering wisdom teams up with you will lend His support and will then team up to bring forth the answers to your questions. There is nothing hard about this matter.

The writer wonders what the point is to getting so much earth education. We here in this plane realize the worthlessness of much education, for we see with clarity how eternal truth surpasses what earth provides. Yet, the earth society will not recognize the truth openly, only privately. They have what they name "requirements," and they have what they name as the "teamwork of book, teacher and student" approach. The earth honors this method. Earth holds this method as the best there is, but earth enters the judgment in error.

The truth that is here for you, the truth that will be your teacher, your great helper, your wise teammate will be what is most needed by you if you are to properly serve mankind. The God truth opens to your use, but when you must honor earth wisdom, you are put to a great test. What do you do with the earth partnership? What do you do with the entering truth that comes to you from this plane? How do you explain yourself?

The questions we ask have answers, dear reader. They are not presented to give wonderment. They are presented to teach you the fundamental understanding you need to be the most successful person possible. Therefore, heed the answers.

The answer to the first question is obvious. The work that you must do there (on earth) to meet requirements is your passport to the earth people and institutions. This passport is what you must present in order to be accepted among

146

those who heed earth truth. But you need not think too well of this passport to your work. No, you need not honor its value more than you honor the One Who is your Source of Wisdom.

The second question is easy, too. The truth that you tune into here is to be used freely, with no apology, no explanation. The way to explain it is simply to announce that knowledge that is intuitive must have a place in your work. "Intuition must be honored," you say if asked. "That which opens the doors of my mind to new wisdom is needed if I am to be all that you, my customer or patient or associate, wants in me." Then, you enter into Pure Truth to know all that there is to know.

At this point, as the writer of these essays, I interrupted the messenger from the Brotherhood to ask about a young man, a plumber, who stated that no one in the city could teach him to be a great plumber. He added that he was learning to be a great plumber by tuning in to a voice within himself. The way he described it, a voice within questioned him, and then he, the plumber, tried to find answers. His questions apparently were the key to his becoming better and better at his work. The response from the advanced spirit was immediate.

The one who expressed that thought to you was open to his own inner wisdom which enters him through the One Who is All-wise, the One Whom we team up with when we want true learning. This young man, the plumber, teamed up with the Source of Wisdom, and this Source gives the man what he needs to become the great plumber he wants to be.

The wonder is that more do not do this continuously, since it is indeed possible!

Is marriage a spiritual bond?

Compatibility is the key, but compatibility is not measured spiritually in the way that you in the earth plane measure that quality. The eternal truth regarding relationships of all kinds teams up with what each person enters life to do. To open oneself to an inferior partership means that the life plan may be hard to achieve, but it is not impossible.

Those who learn of their mistakes in choosing mates must enter into the truth that is just for them. In this way they may know if the situation discourages their potential or not. The truth will enter each one who seeks it to present the true, real or spiritual picture of the marriage relationship.

147

Those who enter into truth will learn a perspective they cannot find in any other way. The teamwork (with God and the helping Brotherhood) will help you become a better teammate to your spouse and a better teammate to the God of the Universe. Therefore, open yourself to attaining this truth. There is no easy way through life's problems. These earth-mind shortcuts will only leave you with the emptiness that earth is capable of giving.

The relationship between two people opens itself to an eternal partnership, but not many accomplish such relationships. Those who have true compatibility probably have teamed up together in other lifetimes, other situations throughout their long period of growth. That they would be together more than once is not to be wondered at because spirit entities usually prefer to join up in various ways to help one another make the best growth possible in a lifetime experience.

Marriage is not a spiritual thing. Marriage is the earth plane alliance that people enter into to provide the new bodies that spirits need. But not only to provide bodies, of course! They marry to provide a base of cooperation—a teamwork that will give help and concern in accomplishing the plans each came with.

Therefore, marriage itself will not be eternal. The relationship between two entities may be eternal, as was explained before. Permanent? What is meant by permanent? The earth plane speaks of permanancy, but in earth nothing is permanent! The spirit is permanent, and therefore, the relationship either develops spiritually or it does not.

The writer wonders about divorce, spiritually speaking I suppose. The means of ending an earth plane relationship is that which is named divorce. But true relationships only bond out of complete tenderness for one another, and marriage has no particular effect on that alliance. The marriage part is to be enacted within the earth plane to satisfy the earth plane requirements that speak of the "home, the family, the eventual bonding of a unit." But marriage, contrary to opinions in earth plane, is not an eternal arrangement made in earth and then continued on the next plane of life.

There are some, as you learned in this book, who still go through the form of marriage they had on earth. But they do this only to help themselves to acclimate to the new plane, the new arrangement here. They open themselves to one another out of habit, mostly, or out of true love. But they will go their own ways eventually to prepare themselves to go on with their lives here or new lives in the earth plane.

People spend much time in this (man-woman) relationship. People rise to new eternal truth regarding relationships or they wither on the vine. Relationships grate and grind when they are not compatible, and people try to smooth away the roughness. But the probable truth is that the entities who search for true mates know innately how to find them.

Others only use earth truth which may suffice to some degree of worth. Either way, people need not stay together if they cannot work through the roughness. They are, however, bound in the way all entities are bound to one another. They who reach out to hurt their mates may not open to any growth in their lifetimes. The eternal truth may show them how to properly dissolve relationships, but the divorce courts of earth only increase the grating and the grinding.

How does aging affect us spiritually?

Those who enter the earth plane know that their time there will be brief. Those who open to an endless life will not be perturbed over whether or not their bodies age, but they will be concerned over a body that sickens and gives no help in expressing truth. Therefore, those who know they are spirit, that their reality is that which will never die, hold the open window of incoming truth to their bodies.

In this way the bodies know how to eternalize or project that which will keep them fit for their lifetime on earth. Those who view aging as precarious and terrible, at best, will project their feelings upon the older bodies even faster than those in younger bodies. The older bodies are quite susceptible to suggestion, and they will unite with truth readily to keep themselves in the light.

But if those who have lost their way in truth open themselves to the suggestions of havoc played in the disease riddled bodies of age, then they will unite with what is poor truth indeed. Those who will turn to light will have lifetimes of teamwork with the Light of the universe. Those who hide from the Light will endanger their bodies.

To be old in human life is to be teamed up with whatever you have been teamed up with throughout your lifetime. Age will not afford you wisdom. The old, old human body is not wiser through experience. The body is only old. No, wisdom comes forth through the use of truth.

Those who view the period of lifetime experience called "old age" with emptiness and with projections of grief and

149

sadness will indeed receive what they hold in mind. But those who abandon the body to live within the spirit will hold the body up to greatness. This may seem paradoxical, but it is truth indeed.

No one who enters truth will team up with the earth-mind axioms of old age. No one who lives by truth will believe the body has its claim upon the spirit. Those who wrest their truth into the earth life know that the spirit/mind holds the answer to all of life's tests. The questions may sometimes appear very deep and very complex, but the answers come in simple terms that anyone can understand.

Do animals have spirituality?

The one who will speak on this subject is a specialist on the energy that expresses in animal form. This entity knows just how each animal may team up with that which is of God, not in the way that people team up with God, of course, but in the way that animals who seek perfection team up. This one works with animal energy to help it develop on this side that it may express well on the earth plane side.

He eternalizes each form that he is responsible for, and in that way he helps that form to develop its potential. The way each animal form develops depends on its willingness to be helped by this entity or other entities here who work with this matter. Therefore, to get answers about animals and their close relationships to those spirits who team up with the God of the Universe, we introduce Peter, the One Who Helps Animals.

My job is to help the development of the animal energy forms. That which presents the personality in each animal is the energy with which I and others work. The reason I chose this work is that I enjoy the creative energy of these who catch the light and express themselves in such myriad fashions. The energy forms I work with now are those of the gentle beasts which offer their energy for development. This energy may express as the tall giraffe or the tiny penguin. It may enhance the life of the giant cats or the tiny one that lives with mankind. The energy is what I concern myself with, not the touch of physical clay that transforms this greatness into earth form.

The energy that I work with wants to advance to whatever it may become, its potential greatness. Therefore, the energy and I work together to make that happen on this plane. They always choose to express over and over on the earth, and they return in one form or another to enhance their teamwork with the light they bring into their beings.

New thoughts enter into these forms as they advance. They enter into relationships without great fear or without aggressiveness. They are the best of the beasts because they work with us here to enact that goodness within them.

The golden retriever this writer has is the energy of one who used to entertain people by throwing up her body and her trunk in a circus that went across the land. Her being loved the laughter, the children who gathered around, the applause. The one who entered life this time as a golden puppy wanted to be part of one of the families she saw there, wanted to receive affection and wanted to give pleasure as best she could. That is the nature of the one you now call Peaches.

The animal forms on earth bring their own worth to the land. They open their energy to do their part, whatever it is. They sometimes fail in this plan, even as people fail. They enter with the idea of growth, but many then team up with the energy of earth that presses upon them. They become the poor truth in expression, even as mankind may become the poor truth in expression. Therefore, the pets that we love may become the pets that evidence hostility. Or selfish or pernicious thoughts may enter them.

Dog breeders work only with the body. They develop a body that is a reflection of the energy that they want to inhabit that form. The energy is attracted to that body because those who breed in this fashion open themselves to receive this gentle energy within the animals. The attraction process is at work here, not the body itself.

Those animals that become so close to their masters that it seems that there is no parting them have the energy teamed up between them. The energy is teamed up to the point that the animal energy wants, when its life form dies, to return to that same person to again be teammates. This kind of teaming up is not strange nor is it impossible. We here on this plane who work with animal energy help that incoming energy to find a body that will certainly go to that most loved person. The energy here is that which is opened to the earth plane for those who tune in.

The explanations were overwhelming, yet they seemed logical. I asked if there is anything about animals that people in the earth plane should know in order to have greater cooperation and sympathy between them.

The energy that enters the bodies of animals enters because it wants to express as that animal. Therefore, never feel sorry for the animal form because it is not, in your opinion, the form that is best. Never enter into the idea that animal energy is any less than your own. The teamed up expression of animals with their spirit selves enters the world as that which is distinguished and proper.

That you should demean any energy is inappropriate for you who are offshoots of God. This energy that enters animals is the teamed up energy of the word of the God of the Universe who put these truth forms into their place on earth. The God of the Universe, in His creative process, provided this energy just as he provided your energy. Therefore, why demean one and not the other?

Nothing that is given to earth must be brought into grossness. Those who express as animals must be given their dignity, their honor, their personal space.

Overview: schizophrenia

Many people suffer from schizophrenia in the earth plane. A psychologist who works full time with such patients asked me if someone from the next plane might shed some light upon the causes and cures of this mental illness.

I queried the advanced spirits from the Brotherhood who put me in communication with a spirit entity who specializes in this mental disorder.

No one entity can shed light on what you seek. Mental problems enter earth life for many reasons. There is no one solution, only many, many problems. Therefore, from here we will give you an overview of entering spirits who have suffered this type of thing.

The worth of a lifetime cannot be given in dollars and cents. The worth of each lifetime experience is what each person must determine for himself. If the spirit cannot adequately express in his body, what use is the lifetime?

Those who work with people who demonstrate mental illness have their hands full trying to sort out the problems. That is why we think that perhaps an overview may be more helpful than the story of one spirit.

There is one category of mental illness that surpasses the others in complexity. That one is what mankind calls the acceptance of what is unreal as compared to what seems real. That, in effect, is schizophrenia. The individual cannot express what others think of as reality. He enters whatever he sees or even hears about as his reality. That way, the problems of the world become his reality.

The schizophrenic individual probably entered life with a plan in mind, a plan to team up with whatever was his reality. But he never defined reality. He gave himself no good definitions, no structure, no pursuance of what is truth and what is not truth. That way his mind fragments what he perceives—fragments it into every true and worthwhile happening that must have merit. But of course that is not right at all. The truth that this kind of spirit wants is what is relevant to his own soul, but he is unable to determine by himself what is relevant. That is why he accepts everything as relevant. Such a one opens himself to too much of the world, too much of earth-mind truth, too much of what is important to others, but he opens himself to very little of what is important to himself.

None of this patient's needs will be as important to him as what he perceives to be his reality out there. Therefore, tuning into his being to help him understand reality is an entirely hopeless undertaking. No one else can crawl inside this person. You, with your understanding cannot fathom the depths of his understanding. You with your wholeness cannot probe the depths of his unwholesomeness. You with your perfection will not turn him into perfection.

The only way to reach this kind of being is through the spirit self, the reality of the being who knows what he is expressing and why. Talk to this one as you would talk to the guiding entity, for in truth, the spirit is the one who guides. Tell this spirit that you enter into the realm of his being, spirit to spirit. Tell this one to be relaxed and accepting. Say that no matter how strange these words may sound, the one you are trying to help is to accept them as truth. These words will indeed help him to be well, to be one who can walk among mankind in full charge of his life.

Express the idea that all this wonderful situation is possible. Then, enter this question: Do you want to get the plan of your life working to make you the wonderful person that the truth can help you be? If the individual enters into silence, wait. Do not talk again, for you may wet down the truth with talk. The patient may begin to think that you bring false words. Therefore, stay silent. Put the words on the table, so to speak, and wait.

If the person seeks further explanation, say to him, 'The temple of your being wants to give you the truth. The greatness which enters you through the open channel to the Universal Intelligence wants to prove itself in your life.' Then the individual will return the answer. Be prepared to receive

'No.' The one in question may say many words, but if they add up to 'No,' then point this out to him. 'You are saying no. I hear a no,' you say to him. Then say that soon you will ask the question again, and leave the subject alone for quite a while, letting his spirit work with what you have said. Never hurry or pressure such a one.

This is the way to work, you see, with gentleness. Once the patient gives the "yes" answer, he will be ready to listen to what you say next. Therefore, you must wait for the "yes." When that affirmative word is entered, you must act with authority. The patient is ready to receive through his spirit self, the only place where real curative work can be done.

Put the truth before this individual by saying, "You are spirit. The spirit self of you is your reality, not this body, this material world." Why? Well, I'll explain it to you.

The body will one day enter into the earth to decay. The earth itself enters into renewal. The buildings, no matter how fine and great, decay and give way to the earth again. The truth of earth is going to pass away too, for it holds only those things that pertain to the body and other material things.

But you, spirit of John or Jane Doe, you will never destruct, never rust, never team up with what is corruptible. Your spirit will survive all possible terrors such as catastrophic illness, dreaded weather storms, the general wear and tear that destroys all materiality. You, the one I am talking to, is incorruptible, permanent, entered into eternal truth.

Therefore, you, the spirit self of (say the name of the person) know what I am saying is true. Pause here for affirmation, for wonderment, for hostility to express. Wait to see which emerges. If no honest emotion rises, then open yourself to repetition of the above. Again, wait. The spirit self, when addressed, enters into self-communion and may be reluctant to send its thought to you. But if you would reach this spirit, you must enter into the energy of this spirit by calling it forth. Wait to hear from it before you go further.

When this one finally expresses, if it be negativity, then let this one know that you are on to the fact that he is hiding within the body hoping not to speak, but you will wait to hear. That it is necessary, in fact, to hear from the spirit self before healing can team up with his whole self. Negativity tells the one helping that there is denial of the eternal part, the spirit.

The spirit will emerge, finally, because it knows you recognize that it is there. 'There is no use hiding,' it says to itself. 'Therefore, I'll announce that I am here.' The person

154

may say, 'Hey, if you want to talk to my spirit, be my guest.' Then he may laugh. But no matter what the response, you have brought that spirit into the open. That's the main thing here.

Now you tell the spirit to listen carefully. Then tell him this: 'The spirit that you are in reality wants to enact his plan for growth in this lifetime. The spirit that you are entered life with a plan that was worked out with the Universal Intelligence. This wonderful plan is within, but the spirit, for reasons known only to that one, has obscured it.' That is the way to be firm, to be totally honest with this one—that he, and he only can make the needed changes, for he and he only created the conditions that he is in now.

An explosion may come because that spirit has been hiding itself, and it may not yet want to be out in the open. Let it posture and shout if it must, but wait patiently. Even walk away or end the conversation. Give your words, but do not hold yourself there for the outpouring of anger. Tenderly put your hands up to stop the outpouring, and smile, if possible. Say, "You will get it all out of your system, we hope, don't we? We know, don't we, that you can be the wonderful person that you visualize yourself to be when you are alone and feeling good?"

Then wait again—wait as long as it takes for the spirit to come forth to talk with authority. This one may react one way; the second one may react some other way. But you, dear helper, must be firm in your work.

When the spirit finally comes forth, come to the point of the conversation which is to instruct the spirit about its work, its power, its authority. Then enter the observation that if this spirit wants to, it can call on that Universal Intelligence itself to help him straighten out the lifetime experience and to make his dreams come true.

As this one develops, talking to you about himself, his desires and dreams, keep reminding him that spirit is in charge, and therefore, spirit can call forth this Universal Intelligence wherever there is a question, a need, a hesitation over acting, a problem, anything! In fact, tell him that soon he will no longer need you because he knows how Universal Intelligence works. It goes inside him if he wants it, if he asks for it, and it will turn him into the entity who stands forth as totally true to his being—the kind of man, or woman, who others turn to as the truth in expression.

EPILOGUE

This is a general plan, of course, but if the helper wants, that one can enter into counsel with us, as the writer does here, to learn more of the personal situation of each patient. Then the helping will be quite fast compared with the accepted procedures of today. Team up with the Brotherhood of God, those noted Counselors on the second plane of life who will help you to deal with those who find themselves out of tune with their physical world.

The God-Mind Connection

An account of the author's communication with spirit counsellors called The Brotherhood, this book provides instructions on finding and making your own personal God-Mind connection. The first volume of a powerful trilogy, Jean Foster's book offers clear information on how to discover your true purpose and destiny.

176 pages, perfect bound, $8.95

The Truth That Goes Unclaimed

In this second book in "The Trilogy of Truth," after *The God-Mind Connection*, Foster explores in detail the specific steps the reader may take to establish his personal God-Mind connection and allow it to be a powerful force in his own life: how to clarify goals, form a correct God-image, build the Inner Temple, and experience truth in practical ways.

176 pages, perfect bound, $8.95

Eternal Gold

In a trilogy that helps readers claim the perfect truth available to each of them in everyday life, this final book reaches forward into powerful new concepts and methods for enhancing life in every respect. Here the reader is shown how to deal directly with God and thus to address problems of health and prosperity as well as individual issues. The ETERNAL GOLD are the truths each one may claim, making life truly richer and more blessed.

176 pages, perfect bound, $8.95

Jean Foster is an important new writer, a very clear channel and one of the many now appearing to show the way to the New Age. Jean Foster's first three books, *The Trilogy of Truth*, have presented an introductory exposition of spiritual principles and have earned her an enthusiastic following. Her next trilogy, *Truth for the New Age*, will begin in the Spring of 1989 with *The Truth That Must be Told*.

In the meantime, we at Uni★Sun will do our best to publish books and offer products that make a real contribution to the global spiritual awakening that has already begun on this planet. For a free copy of our catalogue, please write to:

Uni★Sun
P.O. Box 25421
Kansas City, Missouri 64119
U.S.A.